Vere D Hunt

England's Horses for Peace and War

Their origin, improvement and scarcity

Vere D Hunt

England's Horses for Peace and War
Their origin, improvement and scarcity

ISBN/EAN: 9783337221485

Printed in Europe, USA, Canada, Australia, Japan

Cover: Foto ©ninafisch / pixelio.de

More available books at **www.hansebooks.com**

ENGLAND'S HORSES

FOR

PEACE AND WAR.

ENGLAND'S HORSES,

FOR

PEACE AND WAR,

Their Origin, Improvement, and Scarcity.

BY

VERE D. DE VERE HUNT,

Author of "The Horse and His Master," &c., &c.

"North Tipperary" and "Shamrock" of *Bell's Life*.

> "There are times when we are diverted from errors, but could not be preached out of them."
> STEPHEN MONTAGUE.

LONDON:
BEMROSE AND SONS, 10, PATERNOSTER BUILDINGS;
AND IRONGATE, DERBY.
1874.
Right of Translation reserved by the Author.

TO THE COMMON SENSE

OF

THE GREAT BRITISH PEOPLE

THIS LITTLE WORK IS

HOPEFULLY DEDICATED BY

THE AUTHOR.

BOSCOBEL HOUSE,
    REGENT'S PARK,
        LONDON, N.W.

PREFACE.

WHEN a man finds himself, from any reason, the exponent of an honest and meritorious cause, he need not be choice of words, nor punctilious of demeanour in urging it. Nevertheless, the Author feels all the difficulties that beset this his present effort in its handling. Fearful that enthusiasm in his task might engender a style bordering upon the didactic (so offensive to most readers on equine subjects), and, apprehensive that a less vigorous style of writing might suggest weakness, he has thrown to the winds everything like anticipation of what would be thought of his production in any sense but that of *practical utility*. And, with this slight explanation, he respectfully and earnestly commends the common sense wisdom of the principles he advocates and upholds to the Nation, at a *specially exigent period*, for its consideration.

THE AUTHOR.

Boscobel House,
    Regent's Park,
        London, N.W.

ENGLAND'S HORSES,

FOR

PEACE AND WAR.

CHAPTER I.

So much has been said and written, if little has been done, regarding our general horses, their propagation, improvement, culture, supply, insufficiency, and dearness; to which catalogue we ought to append an alleged decadence, that the subject has fairly passed through that amount of exciting ventilation and publicity which leads to popularity in the public mind.

Writers of varied classes of opinions have dealt with it through works of standard literature, and the medium of the press and periodicals. Men capable of handling it in its varied ramifications and details have devoted energy and ability to exhaustive essays for the last quarter of a century on the subject of our general and military horse supply. From such utilitarian and highly commendable efforts, we have at length aroused the consideration of the great and powerful, without, up to the present, any result beyond that of incontestable practical confirmation of the warnings of writers on the subject.

The Royal Commission granted upon Lord Rosebery's motion in the House of Lords, have discovered, with mathematical accuracy, the inadequacy of supply to our demand; but, unfortunately, nothing has been yet done, or suggested, to rectify so alarming and inconvenient a state of things.

Observations at such a juncture, submitted for public consideration and appreciation, will be rigorously expected to have their base, at any rate, in sound and rational premises. For this is a subject of importance so overwhelming as to embrace considerations of the maintenance of our national supremacy in the future; and that is sufficiently absorbing 'to all patriotic Britons to sharpen their interest and curtail their patience. Something capable of being shaped into practically successful results is what the public now seeks, and anything short of this would be regarded with disfavour. Nor is this state of feeling to be wondered at in the days we have fallen upon, when the most strenuous efforts of the constituted officers fail to keep our cavalry and artillery strength in horses up to a *peace footing*! At the time, too, when a recent enquiry, with all the ægis of Royal Warrant, failed to do more than substantiate the truth of previous assertions as to an alarming want of supply in our military and general horse stock; being admittedly unable to offer any suggestion calculated to prove practicable and popular for bringing about a cure. A Titanic and very recent war, at our doors, has given to the present and future, in the pages of history, powerful illustration of the value of cavalry operations in modern warfare. A recent French writer, too, calls attention to the same consideration in a pamphlet addressed to his Government, urging the necessity for increasing the means for propagation of horses suited to military purposes, and to the unquestionable superiority of the German cavalry, due, as he maintains, almost entirely to *the quality of their chargers*. And this, notwithstanding the fact that France, with her three and a half millions of horses, has at least a million more than Germany. The inferiority of the French horses he attributes (properly, there can be no physiological doubt) to the want of careful selection as to sires of unquestionable attributes, as in other neighbouring states. Prussia has two thousand stallions, or nearly so, in the Government military studs, or *haras*; Austria has more, and all selected by one of the finest judges in the world, well known and much-liked in this country by all breeders and owners of high-class stock; Hungary can count as many; while Russia has the vast number of six thousand horses for re-productive purposes. And be it borne in mind, that these are all animals carefully supervised by competent and duly commissioned officers capable of weighing the merits and demerits of each candidate for the duties of the harem. It is only by comparison we can judge of anything; Government *haras*, under the ablest supervision that careful selection can command, have been found to work well in other countries, where there is not so much sentimental respect paid to private enterprise when national interest hangs in the balance. The French, like ourselves, have discovered a rent in their armour. They wisely make an attempt to repair the injury; we, with characteristic insular apathy and procrastination in anything that costs money and trouble, gravely shake our heads and put our hands in our pockets, not to pull out the needful for the regenerative efforts we are forced to own are too sadly required, but, as a lazy fellow will do, while he contemplates something requiring prompt exertion that he has not the energy to tackle. But it is worse than useless in so regarding this admitted national calamity; for, like the stiff fences we meet with the fox-hounds, the longer you look at them the bigger they get. Those who go at them with pluck and in good form getting off much better than the timid and the shirkers.

Our Gallic neighbours are considering the subject of careful selection of sires and an increase in the number maintained throughout that country. A proposition is now before the French Assembly, that the number of sires should be added to by one hundred annually, until the aggregate supply doubles its present number of stud horses. Considering the immense demands that the resources of France have recently sustained in comparison to those upon our plethoric exchequer, their scheme for increase and improvement of their military horses contrasts favourably with the results of THE LORD'S COMMITTEE on the same subject in England, which, after sitting for several months and exhausting every possible channel for enquiry and information on the subject exercising their research, eventually decided that our supply was not by any means equal to our wants, but that they could not help *that*, nor could they suggest a feasible and popular remedy.

We have now, through the accident of change in the administration, a Government in office, amongst the traditional repute of which is recorded strong sympathies in maintaining our national power and prestige amongst the nations of the earth; and, also, to be favourable to all the interests of our horses, hounds, turf, and other time-honoured institutions. The sympathies of the Conservatives, it is to be hoped, will promptly lead to the consideration and practical treatment of a subject so popular and imperatively important.

We cannot be said to be at peace now, and we are not at war with any people where cavalry forces are required. But can we hope in the course of things to be exempted all through the future from collision necessarily demanding large cavalry aid! Should that day come before our long censurable apathy as to the efforts to prepare for it will have admitted of preparation, where are we! With European ports shut, our horse-breeding colonies too far removed to aid us in horse supply at an exigent moment, and, with our internal resources in that way admittedly inadequate, after the most minute investigation on the subject; may not every Englishman ask, with a laudable anxiety, what is to become of our cavalry and artillery? Cannons, ammunition, and war material that can be made, manufactured, or subsidized, will, doubtless, be forthcoming at the hour of sore need; but let us, as a rational people, remember that we cannot put our looms, foundries, and steam-power to "turn us out" horses; nor are they by any means a portable merchandise, if even opportunity of purchase from any source offered. It takes five years, at least, to mount a dragoon with any reasonable hope of even an approximate amount of that training and endurance essential to a cavalry charger to meet with efficiency the duties devolving to his share through the evolutions and hardships of modern warfare. And five years must only be expected to put us in possession of immature "remounts," by no means reliable under the trying ordeals of a protracted campaign. With such unanswerable difficulties staring the country in the face, how, in the name of the very commonest common sense, is it that if we have no better plan of operations to pursue we do not follow that which has in other states been found to work with practical success? The Government interposition has been a success upon the Continent; with greater indigenous advantages, why should it not be, at least, equally beneficial to us now in our extremity? Let us not shirk the palpable induction, it is no longer a question of *principle*, but of *coin!!*

The following notice of operations of that great cavalry

power, Austria, from one of the leading daily papers, is an exemplification of the attention such matters obtain upon the Continent, while here—well, "the least said the soonest mended."

"Although French horses have but recently made themselves a name, and even yet Frenchmen have but an indifferent reputation in this country for their powers of horsemanship, strange to say there always has been in England a very strong feeling of respect and admiration for the riding qualities of Hungarians, whose prowess and deeds of daring in war have long been celebrated. The gallantry of Edelsheim's Hussars has almost become a proverb in Europe, and the now far-famed Uhlans honestly avow that they learnt many of their arts from the example set them by their gallant enemies of '66. From time immemorial, whatever may have been the defects and failings of Austrian armies and of Austrian generals, no faults have ever been found with their cavalry, and but few with those who led it; while times out of mind have these gallant cavaliers snatched victory out of the hand of the foe, or, as on the bloody field of Koniggratz, saved from utter destruction the remnants of a routed army. We are sure that our readers will be especially glad to learn all the valuable details relating to horse-breeding in Austria that have been placed at their disposal by Lieutenant Colonel Goodenough, our military attaché. In common with our other representatives at foreign courts, he was requested to collect information for Lord Rosebery's committee, and we find the result of his enquiries embodied in a carefully written dispatch, which appears in the appendix of the blue-book issued by the committee. We are likewise indebted to a speech which Colonel Goodenough made on the same subject at a meeting of the United Service Institution last March.

"As our readers are probably aware, Austria, although nominally one empire, under one Emperor, in point of fact possesses two governments and administrations, distinct and independent. As in other matters, so in horse-breeding, the governments of

Austria and Hungary legislate each for themselves, separately and independently. Both encourage 'systematically' the breeding of horses; in Austria there are two, and in Hungary three government studs. A fourth also is soon to be added in Transylvania. In each stud there are from two hundred to four hundred mares, and from ten to twenty stallions, of almost all descriptions of breeds. 'At present every endeavour is made to keep these races distinct, and to send the largest proportion of each to those parts of the country where they are found, by experience, to do best. The produce of these studs is weeded out, and the animals not considered fit for breeding are sold by auction. Out of the best, mares are apportioned for the studs themselves, and the stallions are sent to the depôts, from whence they travel the country in the season, and serve the country mares on the payment of a small fee from 2s. to £10.' In return, however, for the services of these stallions, the Austrian government, unlike the Prussian, has no claim whatever, on the produce, which remains the exclusive property of the owner of the mare. The extent to which farmers profit by this assistance from the State may be judged by the fact that the Hungarian government owns 1786 country stallions, and the Austrian 1600. By a recent census the horses in the two countries numbered 3,525,000. Colonel Goodenough adds, 'The government seeks to further stimulate the breeding of horses by giving prizes to owners of the best stock; in every country district there are annual horse shows, at which commissioners, specially named, attend, and award medals and prizes in money for the best mares with foals, and further, for yearlings, and for two-year-olds, and for three-year-olds. About £2,000 is devoted to this purpose in the Austrian provinces this year. The government also subsidises the owners of covering stallions for each such horse examined and approved by them for breeding purposes; the animal has to be produced annually, and £10 to £30 is then paid on his account.' The above appears to be the summary of the assistance afforded by the Austrian government to private breeders, and from all accounts some such artificial and extraneous aids are much needed, since not only are the peasant farmers in Austria comparatively uneducated and inexperienced in horse-breeding, but the climate in that country is for the most part far less suited for rearing young stock than in England.

"While, however, the general measures adopted by the Austrian government for improving the breed of horses are on the whole simple and apparently efficacious, their military regulations for the formation of reserves are complicated, and would seem scarcely calculated to attain the object for which they were framed. About a year since a new horse conscription law was passed, of which the following are the principal provisions:—
'The whole country is divided into levying districts, and one or more central places of reception are appointed for each. Every year the War Department communicates to the civil authorities the number of horses which would be required to complete the army from a peace to a war footing, on the basis of the existing organisation or *ordre de bataille*. On the basis of this information, the Minister of Agriculture, who is aware, from reports annually received through the district prefects, from the chiefs or overseers of parishes, of the number of horses of different classes to be found in each district, which are also classified according to their probable fitness as riding, draught, or pack horses—apportions to each district the number of animals it has to furnish. At the commencement of each year commissioners are appointed to each levying district, consisting generally of the civil prefect or his deputy, a field or other officer of the army or landwehr, and a veterinary surgeon, whose ultimate duty it is to pass horses into the service. Each commission is assisted by three sworn valuers, experts, chosen if possible from agricultural or other societies. On a mobilisation being ordered the War Department announces the number of horses required, and the time when they are to be delivered, and the civil authorities summon all owners to bring their horses over four years of age to the levying centres. Certain horses are exempted from levy, such as those belonging to the Imperial

family, or which servants of the State or postmasters are obliged to keep to perform their duties, those belonging to public breeding establishments, also all licensed stallions and brood mares certified as such. The passing the horses into the service then begins; those are first taken which the owners are ready to part with for the ordinary remount price of £25; the remainder are inspected, and those which are adjudged fit for service are valued by the valuers attached to the commissions, and this is done without reference to the remount price or to the possibly temporarily enhanced prices occasioned by the mobilisation. The horses valued are then passed into the service, commencing with those of lowest adjudged value, and the owners are immediately paid their price in cash. . . . . To lighten the burden of this forced levy, the parishes of a district are permitted to avoid compulsory furnishing of horses, by voluntary presentation of their proper contingent from their own district. In this case they are paid the remount price augmented by ten per cent., but the horses must be produced within forty-eight hours of the receipt of the order to furnish them. Whilst the levy is going on the owners must keep their horses at their own expense; but the government officers must not detain the horses over forty-eight hours at the levying centres. Thus, if everything is in order, it may be estimated that the War Department would be in possession of the horses they require at the levying centres within four days of the receipt there of the order to furnish them. It is worthy of remark that the major part of the horses thus to be furnished would be destined for artillery or transport purposes, as the cavalry regiments, forty-two in number, are kept up during peace to their full field strength, six squadrons of 150, or 900 horses each, to which is only added, on mobilisation, a first and a second reserve squadron.

"In addition to this system for providing a reserve of horses, as so clearly explained by Colonel Goodenough, there is also in Hungary a description of landwehr answering, in many respects, to our yeomanry. These number in all 32 squadrons, and each keeps up a permanent cadre for purposes of training, but they also buy a certain proportion of horses in excess of their peace establishment. These animals are trained at head-quarters, and are let out to farmers on the condition that they are to be available if required. Colonel Goodenough adds, 'I have myself seen these horses when called out for manœuvres, and I believe that the system has worked well up to the present time.'

"We have placed the Austrian system of providing horses for their army in considerable detail before our readers, as we consider that the newest solution by one of the most military powers in Europe of a problem which has puzzled, and still continues to puzzle, our most able soldiers is deserving of a very full examination. At the same time it is impossible to avoid detecting many flaws and weaknesses in any system which is so complicated, and apparently would require far more than the calculated time to be carried out. We all know the confusion which, in nine cases out of ten, arises on a declaration of war throughout all the departments of any government, however well organised. If all goes well, within four days after the order for mobilisation has been issued, the horses destined for service of the state will have been selected, but it must be remarked that even under the most favourable circumstances they will only have been selected—they will not have been told off to their duties, still less will they have been organized or forwarded to the various points where they are required. As an army without transport cannot move, and without artillery cannot fight, unless some great alteration is introduced into the system just explained we should have much solicitude for the safety of an Austrian army during the first few weeks of a campaign, if it was opposed to an active and energetic enemy like Germany. In a country where distances are great, railways few and ill-organized, the four days wasted in selecting horses might make the difference between safety and ruin. Of course, any such system of forced conscription is wholly impracticable in England, and unless in case of invasion would be quite unnecessary. The practice, however, of letting out surplus cavalry horses to farmers has often been suggested, and is, we think, deserving of consideration, more especially if the principle of localization is ever to be extended to the cavalry."

CHAPTER II.

My object is to lay before all who prize the horse, from a love of the animal, or from sordid or prudential motives, my views as to the great danger in which we stand of really losing him altogether as a sound and useful animal, because of the many causes that have been for years progressively co-operating to deteriorate that class of horses from which we derive many hunters, our hackney and harness horses, and, we may say, all our re-mounts for cavalry and mounted Artillery. I shall endeavour to point out the causes from which a numerical as well as physical falling off in the supply and its character has taken place, and the means which I fancy would, as effect from cause, eventually put things right again.

As nations, like individuals, are capable of deriving benefit and wholesome instruction from example; considering England's long and censurable apathy with regard to that middle or half-bred class of horses that in past time she so successfully and ardently founded and maintained, a reference to a similar national crime or folly, in connection with a like subject, by no less a power than that of ancient Rome, in the plenitude of her greatness, and its decading consequences may be worth contemplation here. At least, the example is not without its most suggestive moral. The students of equine literature need not be told that I owe my following facts to authors of established repute.

Rome found herself, when at the zenith of her power, in possession of a famous breed of horses adequate to the varied domestic duties of a peaceful existence, as well as to the more important and arduous exigencies of war. What the accident of circumstances and the practical policy of other powers, over which supremacy in arms had given her dominance, had placed at her command in the way of horses, she permitted to deteriorate, and censurably neglected any system of improvement, or supply of a, no doubt, valuable race of horses for their times and necessities.

As from the Roman Invasion of Britain it is obvious the native breed of these islands derived a direct and important "cross," it will be well to glance at the sources from whence the *stock* importing the primary blood and form of our horses was derived.

Fable and obscurity wrap the origin and early history of the horse in mysticism. According to the Mosaic text, Asia has given to him, as to man, and all animals that had their prototypes in the Ark with Noah and his family, their original existence. Sixteen hundred years before the advent of the Messiah it is recorded that the horse was used in Egypt. Zoologists acquaint us that the *Equidæ* are traced over a very vast surface of the OLD WORLD— from the West of Ireland to Eastern Tartary, and, from the POLAR REGIONS to South of THE HIMALAYAS, and to an unexhausted distance in Northern Africa. They argue with every show of reason that, because their remains are found in a fossil state co-existing with the *debris* of other animals of a former zoology, that they must have existed in the distribution of a period anterior to our own. A pertinent inference as to the high order of the animal horse in the creation's scale resides in the fact that, while other genera and species with which his fossilized remains have been discovered have ceased to exist, or have removed to higher temperatures, the horse, in our time, alone of these, is to be found in the same regions, and apparently, without protracted interruption; since, from the circumstances which manifest deposits to be of the earliest era in question, fragments of his skeleton continue to be found and traced upwards in successional formations of the earth's strata to present superficial and vegetable mould. Learned philological and other abstruse enquiries, conducted by the ablest authorities, give us only a reasonable deduction upon which to base the opinion that the original horse of South-Western Asia came in a domestic state from the North-East. Hence the first mention made of domesticated horses is coeval with the patriarch Jacob's death, when chariots and horses went up with Joseph when his father's body was carried for burial in the cave of the field of Machpelah. Is it too much to suppose that with Jacob came horses to Egypt? For he came from ON (the Greek HELIOPOLIS), the country of the graziers, invaders, and charioteers from High Asia.

In those remote times, anterior to the domestication of the horse, colonization was of slow and gradual advance, and military conquest restricted to mere vicinity. With commendable alacrity, SESOSTRIS availed himself of the horses of the defeated shepherd invaders, and with those—the first brought to Egypt—he, in turn, passed eastward, to the very sources from which they had issued. From his era horses have been used in Egypt, but that they were numerous in the ranks of war then is doubtful; for, until the time of Joseph, as alluded to, they were unnoticed, and even though at that time the shepherd Scythian invaders of Goshen had been expelled, horses were alluded to as of recent and novel introduction. Even so far on as the exodus of the Israelites from Egypt, it is recorded that, in the pursuit of the Red Sea, the Egyptians could only call out at short notice six hundred chariots of war—"all the chariots of Egypt." Little reliance can be placed in profane historians, and poetical records are not history; but the treatment of the Centaurs, the characters of themselves and horses, though evidently fabulous, lead to a reasonable deduction of a race of horse-men and horses from a basis of truth wrought into imagery and fiction. These fabled beings, but, doubtless, cavalry invaders, belong to the earliest descent of mounted hordes from Central Asia upon Thrace and Thessaly by North of the Black Sea. and across the Lower Danube. It has been inferred that the fabled Centaurs were, in reality, the bold horsemen of the northern Scythæ of High Asia. The period of this raid or invasion synchronises with the heroic age of Greece, and is sufficiently near the periods of the expulsion of the Grazier or Shepherd invaders, the invasion of Asia by Sesostris or Rameses II. and III., and the Indian Epic legends, to establish the epoch of great movements through all the regions in question, and fix the period when horse, chariot, and rider first make their appearance. But it is worthy of notice here that (in Genesis xlix. 17) there is an anterior evidence that riding was not unknown in the days of Jacob —"An adder in the path, that biteth the horse's heels, so that his rider falleth backwards."*

Although it has been attempted to confer upon Africa the honour of having supplied to Egypt horses, in an almost wild state, for subjugation and use, still, from the fact of there being no true indigenous feral horse in Africa, and as the current of human civilization did not certainly set in from Africa to the North-East, while Egypt was not a country for wild horses when the domesticated first appeared there, and that the elements of progressive cul-

---

* NOTE.—I acknowledge my obligations to Colonel Smith and other authors.

ture were taken from Asia, whence the people came, and to which alone they acknowledged affinity, to Asia it is reasonable to attribute the horses of Egypt, and those countries deriving their horses or "cross" from them. But, even in Asia there was a difference respecting horses; for ever since human records began, the male, and occasionally the female population have used the saddle in the northern half, while in the southern it is only within the commencement of profane history that the better classes are mounted and riding tribes, having preferred swift camels, as the Kyale Arabs do to this day.

Want of more accurate geographical knowledge of the territorial limits of primitive Arabia and ancient Egypt, tend to mislead the enquirer regarding the horses in either. A large portion of Western Persia, all Palestine, and Eastern Syria was occasionally claimed within the boundaries of Arab sway in ancient times; and, since the Hejira, they have extended, Eastward, far beyond the Euphrates, and, West, to Morocco. Likewise ancient Egypt at times claimed part of Arabia, of Syria, and the whole of Palestine. Buffon, who asserts that wild horses have been, and still are found in Arabia, with even the wide margin of territory that above facts allow, must be held as in error, for it is argued that "all the peninsula and the provinces that can by any extension be claimed within the limits of the country, have been tenanted from the earliest periods by wandering tribes grazing camels, goats, and sheep, on every space that produced verdure; and there are, nowhere, districts sufficiently inaccessible, or cover properly qualified to shelter horses in a wild state." The probability that there were no horses in this barren and inappropriate region until the period of the Scythian conquerors, or Shepherd Kings, who brought them from high Asia, and left behind them, with many words of their language, their horses, when they had been either immolated or expelled, is the impressive argument set up to show that the Arab horse of the past and present is, like our own thorough-bred, an artificial animal, dependent for his intrinsic qualities to the accident of climatic influence, domestic treatment, "crossing," and judicious culture.

To ancient Egypt has been awarded, by philologists, the first systematic attention to rearing and improving breeds of horses.

That from the Egyptians, Persians, Armenians, the Arabs first derived the horse is, no doubt, correct. That they cannot claim an indigenous horse at *any period* researches of a very exhaustive character have, at various times, been advanced to show. But, at the time of their uniting under the sway of the KORAN, they had for long, as a nation, been accustomed to horses, is evidenced by the manner in which their marvellous cavalry conquests were enforced over the enormous mounted armies of Sassian Parthians, and the disciplined science of Eastern Rome. We read:—"None but a people long possessed of numerous and well trained chargers, could have given wings to the sword of Islam, and in sixty years planted its victorious banners on the Pyrenees, as well as on the banks of the Ganges."

With the extended conquests of the soldiers of the crescent flowed throughout Southern Europe and the far East that strain of *equine* blood, derived originally through the ancient Egyptians, Parthians, and Armenians from high Asia, after long periods of careful culture and "crossing" had improved the animal type that represented it.

The important correspondence that the interest for our present subject has led to in the columns of the *Times* and other journals, gives us, from the scholarly pen of the EARL OF WINCHILSEA AND NOTTINGHAM, the most able letter it has been my good fortune to read upon the Arab and Barb strains of blood to which we owe so much. In reply to one of Admiral Rous's didactic and characteristic philippics his Lordship writes in the *Times*, Saturday, March 7th, as follows:—

ADMIRAL ROUS ON THE TURF.
To the Editor of THE TIMES.

SIR,—It is with some reluctance that I pursue this subject, interesting though it be, because I am persuaded that it is impossible for me, by any amount of proof, to convince the Admiral that he is in the wrong.

He says "Barb" and "Arab" mean the same thing: and so, I apprehend, as far as he is concerned, they always will.

He is the Ofellus of the Turf:

"*Nauticus, abnormis sapiens, crassâque Minervâ.*"
"A fine old tar from whom surprises come,
"Who deals in mother wit, and rule of thumb."

It is not, then, with his stores of information that I would quarrel, but with the conclusions that he draws from them, and the summary fashion after which he disposes of difficulties which appear very great to others who, like himself, have for many years studied the questions of which he considers himself Lord of the Manor.

I shall confine this letter almost entirely to considering whether the Barb and the Arab do, in fact, mean one and the same thing. In my first letter I met this assertion with a broad denial; and I shall now give some of the reasons which have led me to that conclusion, to which I must still adhere in spite of all the prestige and authority of Abd-el-Kader. In fact, I cannot accept Abd-el-Kader's assertions as conclusive where I can show that they are not corroborated by other testimony; nay, more, where the balance of history and unexceptionable evidence is clearly against them.

It seems to me that the Emir's account of the Barbs being, in fact, pure-bred Arabs (see his memorandum addressed to General Daumas in reply to the latter's enquiries) is much upon a par with the Nejdean tradition of Solomon's horse. Palgrave, the latest writer on the subject, who travelled through the Nejed in 1862, considers "the greater part of these pedigrees, and still more the antiquity of their origin, as comparatively recent inventions, got up for the market of Bedouins—*i. e.*, Arabs of the Desert—and townsmen." He adds that one of the grooms attached to the stud of Feysul, Sultan of Riad, then chief of the Wahabees, who ruled over the whole of the interior of Arabia from Djowf to Hasa, on the Persian Gulf, and consequently possessed the whole of the Nejed, remarked to him "that Solomon was more likely to have taken horses from us than we from him" —a criticism worthy of a Yorkshireman; but Abd el-Kader deals with this tradition as positively historical, and in some measure founds his theory upon it.

Palgrave says, moreover :—

"I found at Hayel and in Djebel Shomer good examples of what is commonly called the Arab horse; these are for the most part the produce of a mare from the neighbourhood and a Nejdean horse, sometimes the reverse, but never, it would seem, thorough Nejdee on both sides. With all their excellencies, these horses are less symmetrically elegant; their height, too, is much more varied; some of them attain 16 hands, and some are down to 14. From these, purchases are made every now and then by European princes, peers, and commoners, often at astounding prices."

Here I may mention that Burckhardt, who wrote in 1829, says that there are mares in the stud of Saoud, then ruler of the Nejed, for which he had given as much as £650. Palgrave continues :—

"The genuine Nejdean breed *i. e.*, thoroughbred Arab (sire and dam) is never sold; and when asked how one could be acquired, they answered him, by war, by legacy, or by free gift. In this last manner there is a possibility of an isolated specimen leaving the Nejed, but even that is seldom; and when policy requires a present to Egypt, Persia, or Constantinople, mares are never sent, and the poorest stallions (though deserving elsewhere to pass for real beauties) are picked out for the purpose." (p. 309.)

How then are we to suppose that the horses of Zâb (formerly Numidia), of which Abd-el-Kader speaks, are to be reckoned Arabs of pure family—*i. e.*, thoroughbred, both by the side of sire and dam —when it has from time immemorial been the rule of the Nejed (the only district where they exist) never to let a mare go out of the country.

Palgrave goes on to state that "the total of the Nejdean census of horses would not sum up 5,000;" and says, moreover, "that the number of horses in an army is perfectly inconsiderable when compared with that of camel riders; and that in Nejed horses are never used excepting in war or parade."

Burckhardt abundantly confirms this statement, and adds some very interesting particulars. He says (p. 247, *Bedouins and Wahabees*)—

"The Aeneze tribes on the frontiers of Syria have from eight to ten thousand horses; the roving tribes in that neighbourhood probably half as many. To the single tribe of Montefyk, in the Desert, watered by the Euphrates, between Bagdad and Basrah, we may assign 8,000; and the tribes of Dhofyr and Beni Shammar are proportionably rich in those noble quadrupeds; while the province of Nejed, Djebel Shomer and Kasym (that is, from the Persian Gulf as far as Medinah) do not possess 10,000."

He then affirms "that the aggregate number of horses in the whole of Arabia, from the Red Sea to the Persian Gulf, does not exceed 50,000." He states in another place (p. 246) "that out of the united armies of all the Wahabee chiefs who attacked Mahomet Ali in 1815, at Byssel, consisting of 25,000 men, there were but 500 horsemen, mostly belonging to the Nejed and the followers of Feysul, one of Saoud's sons," who, at the date of Palgrave's visit, was Sultan of Riad (the capital of Nejed) and the whole Wahabee country. He states, too, emphatically, that "it is a general, but erroneous opinion, that Arabia is very rich in horses" (p. 246). Now, these statements are amply confirmed by history.

When Mahomet fought his second battle, that of Ohod, with his old enemies from Mecca, his brethren of the tribe of Koresh, he had but 1,000 men, out of which but two were horsemen; his opponents had 3,000 men, out of which 200 were horsemen (Washington Irving's *Life of Mahomet*.)

This historical fact amply bears out both Burckhardt and Palgrave's statements; and it is worthy of observation that, although it may sound to the ears of Arab breeders a fine thing to date their thoroughbred ones back to Rabda, Noama, Wajza, Sabha, and Heyma, the five mares of the Prophet (from which, according to their account, spring the five thoroughbred Nejdean families of horses — viz., the Taueyse, Manekye, Koheyl, Sachlawye, and Djulfe), Mahomet himself usually rode upon a mule, or the camel El Karwa, whose name has come down to us by the direct track of history, whereas the names of the mares exist but in Arabian tradition.

Abd-el-Kader, according to Admiral Rous's statement (but it is not mentioned in his report to General Daumas), says—"The great event which filled Arabia with Arab horses was the invasion of Sidi Okba." Now, Sidi Okba (as Abd-el-Kader calls him) is the Achbah Ibn Nafe el Fehri of history, and he, we know, was despatched by the Caliph Moawiyah (the sixth successor of Mahomet) from Damascus with 10,000 horse to follow up the conquest of Africa begun by Abd-allah Ibn Saâd. He therefore took with him twice as many horses as the whole census of the Nedjed amounted to in 1862. Moreover, he started from Damascus, which lies at the head of Mesopotamia, the district where Burckhardt assures us the tribes most rich in horses (and these not true Arabs, but Arab cock-tails as we may call them) are to be found. It was not thoroughbred Arabs, then, but Mesopotamians, Persians, Syrians, and cock-tails of all sorts that finished by pushing their invasion as far as Zâb—$i.\,e.$, Algeria, or ancient Numidia. Moreover, Sidi Okba came to signal grief, for he was eventually utterly discomfited and slain by Aben Cahina, a native Kabaile chief, near a place called Jehuda, when his whole army was destroyed, and what belonged to them confiscated for the benefit of the conquerors.

Are we to suppose, then, that this was the chosen moment, when everything was confusion, for establishing the pure Arabian breed in North Africa, keeping up the niceties of its breeding, and dating from that special departure the moment from which the native horse of Numidia (the Barb) lost his individuality, and became one and the same with the Arab? It requires no special scepticism to answer "No!"

But Abd-el-Kader, in his report to General Daumas says, further, "that there were invasions of Africa by certain Arab tribes before the birth of Islamism," and hints "that they then brought Arab horses with them, which gives an earlier claim to the Barb to be considered of pure Arabian blood."

This appears to me to be proving too much, and, in fact, begging the question.

Now, all that I think can be safely predicated amounts to this—that a stream of fresh Arabian blood was (possibly through many ages; certainly since the end of the seventh century A.C.) flowing into North Africa, with which the native horse or Barb was crossed, and probably much improved; but this neither justifies Abd-el-Kader nor Admiral Rous in making the declaration that the Barb and Arab are one and the same race, as both confidently assert.

That General Daumas had grave doubts on the subject, or, indeed, was of opinion that the Barb and Arab were of different races, sufficiently appears from Abd-el-Kader's own statement— "You say that you are told that the horses of Algeria are not Arabian, but Berberein—*i. e.*, Barbs." To this Abd-el-Kader replies in a style that reminds one strongly of Admiral Rous— "This opinion recoils upon its holders; the Berbers are genuine Arabs." Compare that with Admiral Rous's dictum in his second letter—"Plaice's White Turk and other nominal Turkish stallions were pure Arabs." Indeed, were they? Show that, if you please, Admiral, but pray do not take it for granted. For my part, I think I have succeeded in demolishing both your and Abd-el-Kader's proposition, that "Barb and Arab are convertible terms," and a little later I hope to dispose of your theory about Turks being "pure Arabs." Abd-el-Kader, not content with enforcing his favourite notion about the horses, goes still further in order to support it; and, I own, astonishes me not a little, for he makes the Berbers themselves Arabs. "Doubt there is none," says he, "that the Arabian horse came with his Arabian rider." Now, as the Emir insists upon it that Arabs and Barbs mean precisely the same thing in horseflesh, he will have to contend that their riders were the same too; but if this be so, what is to become of Jugurtha, and his cavaliers, a great man of whom most of us have heard as much, if not more, than of the Emir himself?

However, seeing the absurdity of this sweeping proposition,

the Emir is obliged to qualify it by admitting "that if all the horses of Algeria are of Arabian blood many have fallen from their nobleness"—thus, in fact, subverting his own theory, "that the Barb is an exotic imported into North Africa from Arabia," and reducing it to some such proposition as this—viz., that the native race has been through many ages crossed, refreshed, and improved by horses coming from the East under the general name of Arabs, the said horses being, to speak strictly, not pure Arabs, but rather a multitude made up of a dozen different species, coming from as many different districts.

Not only General Daumas, but almost every one who has had an opportunity of seeing both Barbs and Arabs, will be of opinion that the races differ. A Barb has a striking resemblance to the English thoroughbred horse, whereas nothing, as far as appearance goes, can be more dissimilar than the Arab. Their action, too, is different. The Barb lays himself out, and gallops like a thoroughbred. The gallop of an Arab is good for a short spurt only, his natural pace being a long lunging trot, which he is said to be able to keep up for hours—nay, days together, under a hot sun, and with little or no food or water. In a race of a moderate length he cannot hope to beat a good Barb, still less an English racehorse, as has often been proved. I myself have seen a Barb which won all the races of his day, and may be said to have fairly "cleaned out the Mediterranean," that stood at least $16\frac{1}{2}$ hands, and was to look at very much such a horse as Wolf Dog, who won the Chester Cup. Youatt also confirms me in my opinion. "The Barb," says he, "is decidedly superior to the Arabian in form, but has not his spirit, or speed, or countenance. When the improvement of horses began to be systematically pursued in Great Britain, the Barb was very early introduced." After mentioning that the so-called Godolphin Arabian was really a Barb, he says, "the Barb alone excels the Arab in noble and spirited action."

There now remains the *Stud Book*, in the first volume of which we find that the proportion of Barb mares therein mentioned as founders of families is to Arabs as two and a half to one. This alone would justify us in calling the English racehorse an Anglo-Barb rather than an Anglo-Arab; but, in fact, there were other sources besides, from which many important families spring—all of them, however, exotic and foreign.

It seems to me, then, that I have sufficiently disproved Admiral Rous and Abd-el-Kader's assertion that Barbs and Arabs are the same thing—firstly, by the testimony of history; secondly, by common repute; thirdly, by Youatt's description; fourthly, by the pages of the *Stud Book;* and, fifthly, by strong and cogent argument.

Now for a word on the subject of those horses which are mentioned as Turks by their contemporaries, but which the Admiral unhesitatingly informs us were, in fact, "pure Arabs." I would ask, why were Mr. Plaice's White Turk, the Byerley Turk, and numerous others, not to be of that race which their name imports?

The Turcoman horses, coming from the districts beyond the Oxus and Jaxartes, no doubt carried their riders, the Turks, to Constantinople, and thence far on into Europe. Are we to suppose that the Turks are Arabs, or Moors, or Egyptians? They were nothing of the sort, neither were their horses. Turcoman horses, says Youatt, bred in the countries north-east of the Caspian, are large—standing from fifteen to sixteen hands high. So were most of the stallions that have come down to us under the *Stud Book* name of Turks. Why, then, are we to suppose that contemporaries should have been so far deceived as to be entirely ignorant of what they were saying when they called one horse a Turk, another a Persian, a third a Barb, and a fourth an Arab? It is far safer to accept their testimony than to summarily dispose of it after a reckless and arbitrary fashion.

Here I may mention that it was always my impression that the Royal mares were imported from North Africa; and Youatt certainly says that they were Barbs and Turks, not Arabs.

From these considerations I arrive at the following conclusions:—

1. That if one must choose an arbitrary title for the English thoroughbred, it should rather be Anglo-Barb than Anglo-Arab.

2. That Barb and Arab are not the same thing.

3. That it is unreasonable to reject the names given by owners and importers to their horses, and to lump Turkish, Persian, and Hungarian horses under one general head of Arabs.

4. That every English thoroughbred is an exotic coming on both sides from some foreign stock, without any cross of English blood in him.

I may be told, perhaps, that these matters are not now of importance, and that as the English thoroughbred has been brought to a state of perfection, it does not much signify by what process of crossing the result was arrived at; but be that as it may, the subject must always be one of great interest to those who are not content to accept results without studying the means by which they have been secured.

CHAPTER III.

When the Romans invaded England, under Cæsar, they found an indigenous wild horse, partly subdued by the inhabitants, and this native animal was known for ages after to roam districts of the island in a perfectly feral state. They ought to be more properly termed ponies than horses; being of diminutive stature, great hardihood, and extraordinary intelligence and cunning.

To the horses of the *Alæ*, or auxiliary cavalry, and other horses of the expedition, we attribute the foundation of that race for which the British islands are so famous. The Anglo-Saxon conquest introduced another "cross." The Romans, in their economy regarding horse breeding, evinced inferiority in judgment and foresight to the Greeks. In a numerous body of their writers, not one felt the importance of advancing the theory of sound and improving principles of horse breeding. They believed in all the superstitions and absurdities of the idle inventions of silly, and ignorant, or vicious people; and were easily imposed upon by dealers. "If proof was wanted of the true appreciation of the importance good breeds of horses are to a state, we shall find it in the absence of all government institutions of the kind amongst the Romans, until taught by the misfortunes this neglect had brought upon the empire. Some such establishments for improvement and supply of "the raw material" were adopted in the Asiatic conquests."

The Norman conquest of England, effected by mounted adventurers from every country in Western Europe, had a marked effect upon the breed of horses in England. At that time the Spanish breeds, so largely indebted to Eastern blood, obtained through the Mahomedan invasion, extended to England, and it is recorded that William himself rode a war horse of that race at the battle of Hastings. The newly-installed nobles, confident that their victory there was greatly owing to their superiority in cavalry, supported horse breeding with zest and vigour. Roger de Bologne, Earl of Shrewsbury, is recorded to have established "the race of Spain" on his newly-acquired estates of Powisland.

In the battle of Hastings, that the horses were of a much lighter description than those of later days of Norman chivalry, may be inferred from the fact that there the knights were not completely clothed in heavy armour that marked a later era, and that their lances were of so much greater lightness at the invasion, than further on, that they admitted of being used as javelins or darts. The inference is, that as "self-preservation is the first law of nature," inculcating to us the most ample means for defensive and offensive action in warfare, the warriors of the Normans would have been more heavily armed in accordance with that natural law and their own physical power, had the abilities of their steeds to carry more weight than they imposed at Hastings, and co-eval with their immediate advent, admitted such a course of action.

That much attention was paid to increased bulk from this time may be entertained from the altered weight of arms and horses in the Crusades.

It is recorded that Lombardy (A.D. 1217) furnished a valuable contingent for increasing the size and weight of the war horse or *destrier* of the knight. It is written:—

"For, in the rich pastures of the Po a race of ponderous *Destriros* had been found." It may have been from a "cross" derived from the descendants of this Lombardian blood and the "one hundred chosen stallions" subsequently imported by King John from Flanders, that our truly noble breed of active dray horses have sprung.

It is, rather, to the introduction of such animals as the two *Arabs* named A.D. 1121; the one, as having been imported by King Henry I.; the other, as having been a gift from Alexander I. of Scotland to the Church of St. Andrew's, at a period when sacerdotal sway was dominant in the land, and entered so largely and didactically into all secular affairs, that we are indebted for a valuable "cross" with the then intermixed breed that successive conquests and a native *feral* species had produced in England.

The minds of the representatives of chivalry, embracing all Nobles and Knights that ruled the land and held despotic sway with the iron sceptre of feudalism, were so enamoured of "great horses," that is, large and powerful ones, capable of bearing the cumbrous panoply of war or *tournay*, that marked the chivalric era of England, that, notwithstanding there are records of the repeated introduction of Turkish and Barbary horses for the purpose of union with the then existing breed of English mares, it does not appear that there was any acknowledged advantage from the "cross" prior to the reign of James I., who patronised horse racing, and systematized the pursuit. Not content with the efforts made through Turk and Barb stallions to infuse more Eastern blood into the horses of his country, he carried his views further and dealt with a merchant named Markham for an Arab horse at the then enormous price of five hundred pounds. In our day we see twelve thousand five hundred guineas given for a sire (Blair Athol). But, even still, the nobility and gentry had a strong predilection for large heavy horses, in which views they were supported by a celebrated member of their own order, the author of two works that to a comparatively recent period have enjoyed the reputation of standard text books on the continent in matters of *menage*, &c. This was the celebrated Duke of Newcastle, a thorough disciple and advocate of the TIGNATELLI school of horsemanship, introduced by the person from whom it takes its name, in the reign of Henry VIII. at Naples, and was the foundation of our present approved system of equitation so ably illustrated by the teaching of Mr. Frederick Allen. The deserved reputation for knowledge and exalted rank of the duke naturally gave weight to his views and counsel. He unfortunately described the Arab horse as "a little bony animal of ordinary shape, not fleet, and good for nothing." This course of action much impeded the wise efforts of KING JAMES, but by no means discouraged them. He bought another horse from a Mr. Plaice, who was subsequently exalted to the position of Stud Master to the wise and utilitarian Oliver Cromwell, from which circumstance, if no more solid existed, a reasonable inference may be deduced, that, a foreign horse imported by one who was considered competent to advance to such a position as Mr. Plaice enjoyed under the Commonwealth, was a good sample of his breed. This horse's name still stands out in proud distinction at the very root of some of the best pedigrees to be traced in the annals of Weatherby, and is known to posterity as THE WHITE TURK.* Soon after this the horsey monarch's favourite—" Steney "—Villiers, 1st Duke of Buckingham, introduced THE HELMSLEY TURK, and subsequently THE MOROCCO BARB was added by Lord Fairfax. Such patronage to a new order of breeding, at least, happily begot for it the all-powerful aid of "fashion,"

---

* NOTE.—See the Earl of Winchilsea's letter to the *Times*, page 17.

and from this period the preceding taste for "great horses" gradually and visibly diminished. Charles I. strongly imbued with the same feelings about horses as King James, gave strong support and countenance to racing, as the most direct goal to the national good for establishment of a desirable breed of horses. Independent of monetary consideration, the Isthmean contests founded in this monarch's reign in Hyde Park and at Newmarket begat a rivalry and a channel for the exercise of mind and money gratifying to the dominant and wealthy classes, that induced to the breeding of that description of steed that, combined with great weight-carrying and enduring powers, the utmost fleetness that could be gained without impairing the other named two great essential qualities. Indeed, we find that one so practical and expert in military matters as THE PROTECTOR himself had discovered that mere bone and stature was no match against action, speed, courage, and endurance; for, all reliable records go to show such was the class of "re-mount" that made his cavalry a singular page in history and brilliant in poesy and story.

At any rate, from his period the matter in favour of Eastern blood seems to have been decided, for, it is the subject of record that at the time of the RESTORATION Charles II. sent his "Master of the Horse" with a strong commission to the Levant, to purchase stallions and mares. Barbs and Turkish horses became frequent, numerous imports to England at this time, and eventually stallions of every breed of the East were grafted on the British horse. To the time of QUEEN ANNE, more particularly since the Darley Arabian era, when the importer of that very celebrated progenitor of our best blood after much opposition succeeded in establishing the Arab "cross" effectually; and in engrafting that race upon the English, thus completing the working of a system, which, under careful management had given us the *desiderata* of speed, stamina, beauty, and soundness up to the period when the results from a *new organization of the racing code of laws* began to show its sad and lamentable effects upon, not only the highest order of horses, but, throughout the various breeds of any importance in the nation, deriving largely from TURF blood.

CHAPTER IV.

THE majority of horses bred in the British kingdoms and colonies for the ordinary purposes of domestic and fashionable life, the chase, and war, are not thoroughbred, but possess a very large and predominant share of stud-book blood; and, almost generally, are derived from stallions the off-spring of the racing arena. It behoves us not here to enter into the question so much agitated as to what particular strain of blood the English racehorse derives his highest attributes from. Arab, Barb, Turk, Spanish, Flemish, German, and Norman horses have more or less contributed to produce this horse as he was, and as he is, under the different influences consequent upon his management and employment. The powers of English racehorses, tested in every country and under every clime, have been proved pre-eminent. It is unnecessary to quote the recorded instances which are so familiar to all readers of literature of this description. It is enough for us to know that by the term *blood*, an eminent writer defines it in horses to mean " the qualities produced in a horse by a superiority of muscular substance, lightness, and compactness of form, united with a justly proportioned shape; or a physical structure of tendon, bone, and lungs, proper to afford the full effects of the mechanical means of speed, when set in motion by high innervation. When these conditions of the problem are fully carried out, by a judicious and persevering course of breeding and education, there will be beauty of form, and the blood will be adapted to such purposes, within the compass of the laws of nature, as were aimed at, provided recourse has been had *from the beginning to select the finest models* for the purpose." Well, so it is, no doubt, and that the practice pursued carefully in these kingdoms for numerous years has produced a type of horse, taking him all in all, never before equalled is, likewise, a truism. I shall, therefore, start with the assumption that at some comparatively recent period, if not now, we had generally the English thoroughbred a representative of blood, substance, bone, power, beauty, action, temper, and fleetness with indomitable endurance. And we must admit that with the stud use of individual examples, approximating in a reasonable degree to this high standard, our pasturable districts in this kingdom and the "Sister Isle," produced a half-bred stock for the supply of the nation's cavalry and artillery, and for ordinary purposes of saddle and harness, of great excellence and reputation. It is also desirable to note here that from causes which I shall proceed to elucidate in the sequel, the same amount of genuine and desirable attributes are largely absent from this important class of England's horses at the present time; so much so, indeed, as to have given rise to much discussion on the subject in two leading sporting journals of weekly issue, and to cause the subject to reach important quarters for ventilation and consideration.

I venture, with the utmost diffidence and respectful solicitude, to attempt to *tone*, if not to educate, the mind of my readers to a harmony with my efforts, by which I would hope for exclusion from the undue weight of preconceived and ineradicable notions arising from strong partiality. I would suggest they calmly received the plaintiff's evidence and his advocate's address, and after weighing all carefully and well, they made up their minds, as they would be supposed to do in a jury box, from pure evidence and fair deductions, rather than from fixed notions upon a basis not in accordance with existing facts, but more as the representative of common report. If I can reasonably show the nobility, gentry, and farmers of this country that notwithstanding there were never at any period finer specimens of the British horse to be found, still, more unsoundness, "weediness," deformity, and scarcity than has previously existed has marked our general horses of late years, I should hope that the fact will be considered, in the face of recent lessons as to the paramount effect of efficient cavalry operations in a campaign, to be sufficiently momentous for the "hereditary legislators" of this country to take in hand and afford that attention and energy to, that any imperial question of similar magnitude and importance should challenge and obtain.

If in the course of our subject the reader is struck with my directing my attention largely to horse breeding and horses in Ireland, it will be just not to attribute the fact to the nationality of the writer; for my long residence in England, and the accident of my singular profession, "calling," or trade, have afforded me so thorough an insight into every phase and bearing of the paddock, the post, and the dealer's operations in England, that an intimate knowledge of the important share that the "Sister Kingdom" bears upon the supply, not only of our military re-mounts, but of the higher class of hunters and other fashionable horses, necessitates a careful review of the facts and circumstances existing in that island with regard to the breeding of horses. Many practical men, through different grades of society there, are friends and acquaintances, who both breed and purchase Irish colts; and from information of a most direct and reliable character, supported by export evidences from that country, warrant the assertion that great numbers of the mature horses that find their way into the stables of the aristocracy direct, or through the medium of the fashionable dealer, have originally come from Ireland into the hands of "horsey" men in Yorkshire, Lincolnshire, and other localities having the reputation of breeding districts. Therefore I feel that in largely directing my remarks to Ireland, I go to the fountain head of the hunting and cavalry re-mount supply, and it is with these my observations should chiefly be connected.

Genuine superior horses never rated so high in market quotations as at present; and it is lamentable to say that this result proceeds as much from the want of supply as from the increased requirements of fashion. There is, unhappily, not only a numerical falling off but a deterioration in power and general soundness of our horses. This is a fact existing and incontrovertible, and no amount of flippant or plausible writing can alter it, although it may mischievously tend to allay public apprehension through that superficial general mistake of taking as correct anything written, with a show of authority, about what we do not perfectly understand. While some deliberate and thinking penman appeals through the medium of widely diffused columns to the support and sympathy of those classes mainly interested, to take active measures to meet what he knows to be an existing and growing evil, other scribes, whose opportunities do not afford them the same general means of enquiry, unfortunately glance only at the select specimens of the thoroughbred horse that come under public notice, and point to those examples in a blatant and jubilant strain, as evidences existing to overwhelm any theory that advances a general degeneracy, and an absolute necessity, if the nation desires and requires to keep its horses up to a sound and effective standard, that their propagation and culture should be based upon sound effective principles, and not entirely left to the exercise of custom or individual taste. Surely it is not because we see sample horses of the grandest type of form and action— " the poetry of motion " itself—that those desirable qualifications are generally apparent. Look at the supply of candidates for prizes at the different horse shows, and those " judges " whose age and experience can run them back to a quarter of a century ago or more, can tell that for every single show horse, or rather prize horse, *now* exhibited, *many* might have been *then*. Look at our cavalry regiments—the lancer and hussar ones have smart active animals—seldom complete in numbers; and the heavy dragoons and artillery inefficiently horsed in quality, power, and numerical strength. Go amongst " the dealers " who supply hacks and harness horses. What represents a majority of their studs? Foreign importations! Not from choice, but of necessity; for they will frankly tell inquirers " there are no horses in the country." Literally, horses are numerous enough, but of that sort which the critical acumen of a good judge would select for the London market, there is positively an alarming dearth.

From that once great prolific nursery for England's war horses and fashionable stable, Ireland, comes mainly and materially this heavy national misfortune. The Committee of the Royal Agricultural Society, appointed to enquire into the reported degeneracy of horses, &c., quotes Ireland prominently, because minute enquiries afford returns with full exemplification, not obtainable at present throughout the great breeding districts of England; and it is well established that a majority of the *superior* horses sold out of the great horse breeding districts in England are animals imported from Ireland at an immature age. It is not, then, Her Majesty's Government alone that is interested in the wellbeing of horse supply and produce in the Sister Kingdom. The gentle being that personifies elegance and grace to the admiring loiterers by the side of Rotten Row on a "full house" day in the height of the season—the acme of attitude and harmony of motion, the bold dragoon, who hopes with a soldier's professional ardour to yet "flesh his maiden sword," the gallant fox hunter, characteristic four-in-hand man, wealthy gentleman, and hard-working tradesman, are all interested individually, as well as from that fine feeling of national pride, so largely pervading the people of this realm, in this all-suggestive and nervous question of degeneracy in numbers and quality of "ENGLAND'S HORSES FOR PEACE AND WAR."

Few commanding officers of cavalry are more competent than Colonel Baker, to give a practical opinion regarding the question of supply and demand in the horse markets; and the following extract from a letter, addressed by him so far back as the 18th November, 1863, to the committee appointed by the Royal Agricultural Society to enquire into the subject of degeneracy in the breed of general horses, may be produced here with suggestive warning and interest. He says:—"The deterioration of the breed of horses in Ireland, must be considered as an evident and acknowledged fact; and it is important that the reason should be traced, and, if possible, arrested. In my opinion, several causes have led to this result:—

"1st—The increased demand for horses, of even inferior quality, which has arisen from the large influx of continental buyers.

"2nd—The carelessness with regard to brood mares and stallions, which is so general amongst the lower classes of Irish breeders.

"3rd—The dearth of good stallions, and the consequent improbability that the poor horse breeder can make use of a superior, but expensive, sire.

"4th—The introduction, generally, of fashionable, rather than sound and useful, blood. My impression is, that this evil admits of only *one cure*, viz. :—the establishment of a stud of well-selected stallions in each horse-producing county; those horses being held at the service of poor farmers of the district, *gratis*, for such mares only as might be considered fit to produce superior stock. Annual prizes might be given for the best colts and fillies thus bred. This is the system that has been pursued of late years, both in France and Austria, with the most remarkable results. How the necessary funds are to be provided is, of course, a difficult question; but the application for a Government grant in aid of so purely national a scheme would, I think, be quite legitimate."

I have only recently, and accidentally, come across this valuable contribution from so thoroughly practical, experienced, and unselfish an authority. I am glad to quote the Colonel's remarks; and the circumstances under which they were called forth are worthy of notice, as tending to suggest the rational inference that the importance of the occasion that produced them, and the character of the body to whom they were addressed, would add additional care and deliberation to the forming and utterance of any opinions. And besides, such evidences may very materially aid our efforts in securing the ear and attention of some "hereditary legislator," not too blasé, or too superficial, to lend that aid which the accident of position gives him the opportunity to use for public advantage, from the circumstance of being heard in quarters from which, at least, would be derived the consideration of a very general publicity of a grievance that only requires to be known and accepted generally to be speedily and efficiently redressed. THE ROYAL COMMISSION has gone a considerable length to effectuate this object; but constant twitting will be needful not to allow the knowledge its efforts has awoke to be veiled from a too frequently hood-winked public.

To effectually eradicate any evil, it becomes necessary to strike at its root. Therefore, with this incontrovertible axiom before me, it is scarcely necessary to disclaim any crusade against racing and its votaries; where in endeavouring to get at that "root," I trench upon the delicately and jealously guarded portals of *the turf.* Be it therefore borne in mind, that I seek not to travel beyond a lament that the grievances of deterioration in our general horses can unmistakably be traced to the pernicious influence of a weedy and unsound type of horse, that the advent of a different system of racing to that which our ancestors indulged in eventually brought into our Isthmean Arena, to be afterwards most unfortunately foisted upon a blood-loving public, through the medium of high-sounding and pretentious pedigrees, enhanced by winning brackets in the records of *Weatherby* and *Baily.*

To our racing stables we may look for the origin of the cause of complaint as to want of as much bone and soundness in the horses of our day for general use as distinguished those of former times; and to the same source let us turn for an explanation, for from them became scattered over the length and breadth of these kingdoms that bane to the improvement and certain begetter of degeneracy in the British or any other horse; the worn out and unsound racer, who, with contracted disease, false action—promoting and fostering false shapes—and when past all "patching and piecing," is too frequently inducted into those duties of progeniture which all physiological examples teach, should, for improvement and perpetuation of excellence in any breed, be intrusted judiciously and systematically to only *the best* and *purest bred* males. Surely from no such objectionable or tarnished source can we with any show of reason expect ought but a stream partaking more or less of the parental or primary influence? Temporarily by some casual counteracting cause it may be rendered delusively pure; but the foreign ascendancy is not always potent enough to be dominant over the main evil. So is it with attempts to counteract the effects of disease or malformation transmitted by an objectionable stallion; for a generation or two you may succeed, but, subsequently the latent defects become, as in the source from which they sprung, a prominent deformity.

We found in the establishment of Royal Plates in the past, when the operations of turfites required a stimulant not afforded them by the opportunities and excitements of our own gambling era, a vastly improved supply of horses of substance and stamina. The money given for these royal plates, with a view to encourage the propagation of blood horses of a superior type, when race-horses were not numerous, and the prizes awaiting their successful efforts moderate, was all fair and legitimate; but the sums expended for QUEEN'S PLATES at the present time could be, in my individual opinion, vastly better employed towards producing an identical object; and this, too, without interfering with the "national pastime" or its votaries to any appreciable extent. There is sufficient inducement to the disciples of the *turf* to continue to breed the best they can, irrespective of HER MAJESTY'S PLATES, which in no instance are now the means of creating those contests which they were inaugurated to engender, and in former times produced. And really any reigning MASTER OF THE HORSE might have been reasonably expected, in common justice, to have given some careful consideration to this subject, so loud does it call for consideration; allowing that the duties of many in high places are deemed too onerous or too prose to admit of more than routine attention, even in exceptional cases crying for redress. The *turf* men have, honestly, no right to complain if the country is awakened to the expediency of withholding a national grant, the objects of which their own private system and speculations have positively and absolutely nullified. Those two-year-old races and handicapping have " put the extinguisher " upon any hopes of good being effected by our gracious sovereign's liberal donations to the sustenance and promulgation of horse-breeding. The inducements for finding out the merits of the race-horse at too early an age are so cogent and numerous as to upset the hope of any promising colt or filly being preserved from the deleterious system of the training stable until a matured frame and indurated muscles might defy it. And a horse capable of contending for Her Majesty's guineas would be spoiled by a brilliant contest therein for the more paying "game " of winning a handicap, so is generally reserved for that.

The tissues of a horse are not fully developed until he is six or seven years old, says a well-appreciated veterinary authority, and, therefore, in a two-year-old, must be naturally weak and slender; in proof of which remember that the ends of the bones (*Ephiphysis*) at this age are not joined by long union to the common shaft, rendering them incapable of resisting the tension imposed upon them by the tendons and ligaments, during excessive action. Nothing interferes so much with the wise laws of NATURE as early training. It is said that "Nature is ever economical in her means and wise in her ends;" but early training frustrates her "means," and, consequently, defeats her " ends." As in the vegetable kingdom, the seed placed in the ground will not be hurried, but has to pass through many stages before the full ear of corn is developed, so in the animal kingdom, the primary cell has to undergo many changes before it is transformed into the particular tissue for which it is destined. Too early training of any kind is productive of incalculable mischief, whether it be mental or physical. It will be found that experience can endorse that every nine animals out of ten submitted as two-year-olds to excessive exertion on the turf never reach the age of five with unimpaired physical powers. The abuse of noble young horses before vigour has established her empire, taxing to the utmost powers which are only artificial and accelerated by a system detrimental to the last degree to the object for which " KING'S PLATES" were first established, is the too patent root of the evil of the want of bone, substance, soundness, and "stoutness," in a large majority of our horses of the present era.

So long as extended courses and *adult horses* were the vogue, we find less injury resulting beyond comparison, than the present system of short gallops and immatured animals has been productive of. The abuse and persecution of promising colts and fillies for the gratification of only individual feelings of pride or lucre, is injurious to the beast, lowering to the man, and detrimental to national wealth, glory, and safety! Ill calculated to do anything but harm to horses, and certainly not elevating to human nature, either morally or socially; a debasement of a utilitarian system that had for its pristine object the elevation and progressive improvement of that general horse stock of the British Isles—the pride and glory of the country, and the envy and admiration of the civilized world. That stock once pre-eminent, and that should have remained so to the end of TIME. Whereas, *au contraire*, it has sent abroad upon the face of the land the worthless and decrepit stud horses, whose very infirmities render them easy of acquisition, and whom needy speculators have, through a resonant pedigree and other superficial lures, imposed upon an ignorant and confiding constituency to whom England looks to maintain, in excellence, her supply of " re-mount" and general horses. Verily! the means justify the end!!

CHAPTER V.

THE majority of our GENERAL HORSES, we all know, are the off-spring of thoroughbred sires. The reason of degeneracy, then, becomes apparent enough. The greatest number, in fact a very great majority, of these stallions are not chosen with regard to the indispensable requisites to success in a country sire, namely, soundness, formation, substance, bone, action, as well as *pure blood!* Without these *desiderata*, the purest bred animal that can be produced is valueless as a progenitor of *general horses*, because imperfect form and such *acquired* defects as the necessities of the trainer's operations engender are, too frequently, transmitted to the offspring. Of those evils, a decrepit frame, "curbs," "roaring," and "contracted feet," most heavily visit posterity; and what more deleterious evils can scourge the general breeder, and punish, impoverish, and endanger a nation having so much material wealth embarked in horses, and such grave considerations depending upon a full and useful supply of them.

If we are only sagacious observers of NATURE'S workings and consistent disciples of her rules, it will require nothing beyond an ordinary degree of perspicuity to discover and adopt the best means of nullifying and overcoming the existing and lamentable products from a pernicious system.

For example, we see a sire with "curby hocks" and contracted feet, the property of a popular owner, in an Irish horse-breeding district. This sire has the favours of over one hundred mares in a season; a majority of his offspring partake in a ratio of three to one of those objectionable qualities that marked their sire. Still the owner, from any cause you please, except the intrinsic worth of his stallion, has gained the suffrages of his neighbours. Things go on so while the horse lives, and, though prudence, common sense, and judgment ought to prevent it, the horse is permitted to entail upon posterity defects calculated not only to punish an ignorant constituency, but to help to bring about that national calamity of degeneracy through our middle-class or half-bred horses, under which the country absolutely groans at present. Our position was not less pardonable than serious, being quite unable to keep up the cavalry "strength" in "remounts" at a time when the painful contiguity of dread wars and political complications were calculated to impress reflections productive of a train of thought upon these subjects, that it is to be hoped in such a country as England, and amongst such a clever, educated, and spirited people, jealous of her hardly and gloriously won supremacy amidst the nations of the globe, will bring about that calm and unbiassed enquiry which anything of such great magnitude, and touching upon national interest and honour, should be awarded. I fervently cling to the hope, notwithstanding the censurable apathy which exists as to the paramount influence of the sire in propagation, and the unguided or ungoverned exercise of individual judgment and interest in his selection, that out of our present richly earned necessities will arise the future salvation of our general horses, and that good wholesome alarm will enlist public sympathies on the side of those innovators who have sounded the tocsin of alarm, and denounced the deleterious system so long and mischievously adopted generally by breeders of half-bred horses.

I read that in the Highland Agricultural Society of Scotland, was opened an interesting physiological problem as to the relative influence of male and female parent in the propagation of horses, which was propounded in this manner: Whether the breeding of live stock be susceptible of the greatest improvement from the qualities conspicuous in male or female parents? A variety of opinions were elicited, and some from names standing very high both as the greatest scientific authorities of the day and as the best practical breeders.

Mr. Boswell, of Balmuto, was on the side that awards to the male the greatest transmissive power; and after an elaborate investigation concludes *that he is the parent to which we can alone look, from motives of sense and sound polity*, for improvement of any stock.

A more modified view was taken by Mr. Dallas, of Edinburgh, who gives his opinion that, while the male is more potent in imprinting *external qualities*, the female is more influential for those which are internal. Hence he teaches that the sire should be selected for improvement of coat, colour, size, bone, action, and general configuration, and the female for hardihood, and, in fact, all purely constitutional attributes.

Mr. Christian, of Mull, takes a middle course, and contends that the offspring partakes of the qualities of that parent which exerts the strongest influence in formation of the *fœtus*, and recommends the selection on both sides of the best animals of the breed sought to be improved that can be found. That such a theory is a very safe one there can be no doubt; but it is by no means so convenient in the breeding of gregarious animals as that which allows to the male a preponderating influence. One stallion may beget in one season *one hundred foals*, while the mare only produces *one*. Therefore, from such an example we can argue that one stallion's influence upon posterity is cent. per cent. greater than one mare's.

Nature, the "universal mother" and unerring law-giver in her own domain, in her untrammelled workings, supports this theory practically, or why should we see in wild flocks and herds that the favours of the females are submissively rendered to that "lord of the harem," who, from superior physical powers and puissance in combat with other aspirants of his sex and kind, has maintained, by individual power and prowess, a determinedly contested supremacy? It may be inferred he is the best, or one of the best of the herd he represents, be he stag or stallion, and that, was there not some innate influence direct from the Creator that impresses his kind with a lasting homage during the period of his ascendancy, animal nature would suggest renewed conflict more generally on the part of those individuals that had been worsted in the muscular and nervine contests necessarily preceding the established sway of the reigning lord. For we see an undefinable law, exercising influence under natural administration, to retain in peaceable and undisturbed possession of his offices that male that has proved himself a peer amongst his kind, and whose thews, sinews, and pluck have placed him in a proud supremacy, entrusted with the transmission of his species. In the face of such a system, resulting from natural laws, what right have we to attempt any digression in application in the propagation of horses for domestic uses and the exigencies of war. No doubt it was a similar course of observation and train of reasoning that suggested to the late Rev. J. H. Berry to record that, *only one rational course can be adopted by breeders*, viz., that of resorting to the *best male*, "a simple efficacious mode of improving such stock as required improvement, and the only proceeding by which, stock already good, can be preserved in excellence."

The well-known examples of those *hybrids*, between the male pony and female ass and *vice versa*, are very conclusive evidence as to the preponderating influence of the male parent in transmitting external organization and appearances to posterity.

May it not, with every show of reason and example then, be deduced that male influence in propagation of gregarious animals is paramount? Such, doubtless, is the case; but the contrary is a vulgar belief; and the general breeders of half-bred horses imagine that a good mare may be put with impunity to any stallion, boasting in his escutcheon a long list of ancestral "flyers" of the turf, not knowing or caring whether he or they were defective in those material points from the propagation of which *alone* can success and satisfaction attend upon horse-breeding as individual speculation, or for the possible period of a great national necessity.

Granting, then, for argument's sake, if you do not from complete conviction—or, probably, from the native insular instinct of calling a thing or system right because one is and has been used to it—the preponderating influence of the male parent amongst gregarious animals in transmitting their individual form and characteristics to their descendants, and it being incontestable that bad qualities are as easily, or, indeed, much more easily transmitted than good ones—for "ill weeds grow apace"—does it not impress those interested in the subject with the very grave importance of having that source from which good or evil must, as a natural consequence, flow, of such character and merit as will insure beneficial instead of deleterious and degenerating results? Surely yes. And all will admit that care, judgment, and forethought must be invariably used in selecting any stallion to improve stock, and that he should be not only full of good qualities, but free from bad ones. For it cannot be too forcibly impressed upon horse breeders that, from the constantly recurring examples in this species of breeding of offspring " throwing back " even to remote ancestors, it is wise to go beyond the appearance and qualities of the immediate stallion about to be selected, and be satisfied as to the soundness and general merits of his ancestors; for, unfortunately, the good or bad points of an ancestor, though not represented in, say a son or grandson, may flash forth in a further removed progeny. Hence, in breeding, the rule supreme is, "like begets like or the likeness of *some* ancestor;" and the *purer the blood* the more forcibly will the characteristics of the individual animal disseminating it be marked upon offspring, always, nevertheless, allowing to the male the superior influence in such particulars.

Imperfect sires beget imperfect stock. Foreign competition and the requirements of breeders for *turf* purposes, monopolize those sires that, properly placed through England's great nursery, Ireland, would be of great service in regenerating that class of horse, the very aspect, character, and qualifications of which are largely departed within recent years. There are a few honourable exceptions, but it may be excepted as a suggestive and unpromising fact, that the majority of stallions available to the great bulk of Irish horse breeders are effete, unsound, and highly objectionable outcasts of the racing stables, too defective to be used in propagation of their own order, and inferior in those material attributes of soundness, "quality," bone, and action that would render them an object of notice to the clever foreign buyers who always hang about the English horse markets. It is notorious that for the last twenty-five years or more, colonels of cavalry regiments, contractors for remount supplies to our cavalry and artillery, veterinary surgeons, and painstaking penmen have been publicly registering experiences tending to exhibit, with a view to correction, shortness of supply in numbers as well as a large and increasing falling off of those "wear and tear" characteristics of a former period in respect of "Our Cavalry Remounts and General Horses."

In Ireland, so prolific a nursery of that half-bred stock from which military horses are derived, the effects from indiscriminate and untutored breeding, continued with certain influences dependent upon political changes within the last quarter century, have made a very serious and sad alteration in the quantity and character of horse supply; so much so that it is alarming to think existing facts in that kingdom, in connexion with the subject under notice, have only recently led to Government enquiry. For I am grieved to say, though in India the very same question of re-mount horses should be deemed of sufficient importance to have, long ago, a carefully constituted Government Board of Inquiry established to "investigate and report," that at home a perplexing and detestable apathy seems to have too long prevailed on the subject, although existing grievances in this department of national economy *shriek* for redress. Yearly recurring evils, long admitted as existing, are permitted by the apathy or want of sympathy in the matter by successive Governments, to run their poisonous and degenerating course; sowing a seed of carelessness and ignorance, year after year, that has rendered in due season an inevitable crop of loss,—individual and national—disappointment, and disgust.

The proneness of Englishmen to put great faith in their insular position and hereditary means of defence against invasion, may be one cause for apathy upon a subject that has so largely influenced the operations of two great military continental powers so recently in fearful conflict. While England has been doing nothing to systematize the means for producing her "re-mount" horses, both Germany and France have devoted judgment, forethought, and lavish expenditure to the economy and improvement of horse breeding. The lesson taught to other European powers by the glorious exploits of German cavalry in the recent Franco-Germanic war, and the great influence brought to bear upon the campaigns by cavalry operations, are too patent and potent to be lost upon any power that may one day be called upon, from any circumstances, to uphold principle, policy, political or individual safety by force of arms. Can England say that she is exempt from such a possibility? If from the records of the past we do not draw inferences and lessons to be turned to advantage in the present, we can only admit that we have drifted into that apathetic spirit that actuated older and equally great powers in their own time, and that so surely heralded their decadence and fall. Let us hope that the shock of conflicting nations still ringing in our ears and appalling our outraged senses, even by memory of the sad events, may be strongly suggestive that the days are not yet come in which a false security, begat by long exemption from the evils of active war, ought to justify the sword being forged into the ploughshare, nor any one thing that can contribute to the strength of the British nation in the time of active strife, being neglected or overlooked.

If Germany and France have, through our open horse markets and ports, had the cream of our best half-bred mares for many years—the very choicest seed for our own crop* of military horses—their recent quarrel has largely benefited the future of horse breeding in the British Isles, if any prompt steps are taken for the supply of judiciously selected stallions throughout horse breeding districts.

---

* NOTE.—Observe in a quotation from MR. EDMUND TATTERSALL, farther on, we have the startling *fact* that from *two ports alone*, in this country, 14,900 of our best mares have gone to the foreigners in seven years!

Many thousands of most objectionable mares have been sent away to fill up the devastated ranks of the French cavalry. Everything now combines to point out the present time as opportune for any effort having for its object Governmental supervision or assistance to the great horse breeding districts, in Ireland chiefly.

CHAPTER VI.

It will readily be remembered that about twenty years ago an act of the legislature entitled "The Irish Incumbered Estates Act, &c.," was instrumental in introducing into that country many English and Scotch farmers. The small fields and light scratchy husbandry of the old native system happily fled before the innovatory lesson of the new comers. Their heavy agricultural carts, ploughs, and other agrarian implements, if calculated to so much advance farming interests, had a materially opposite effect upon the far-famed breed of Irish half-bred horses. Ireland being essentially a tillage country, the size and capacity for draught and burthen of her horses had a dominant influence upon the character of her implements of husbandry that were to be worked by horse-power. For the increased burthens produced by the imported system of agriculture it was considered that a weightier and more cumbrous animal than the native half-bred, active Irish horse was necessary; and in the plenitude of unbridled ignorance the convenient but ruinous expedient was hit upon of crossing upon Irish mares—so noted for a large infusion through various channels of the purest Eastern blood—huge Clydesdale and other ponderous horses. The natural offspring of such a union all physiologists can quickly define. A nondescript brute with a heterogeneous mixture of parts; a large head upon a blood-like neck—a huge elephantine carcase upon insufficient limbs, covered with a coarse and long hair, and quite unequal to the effective carrying of such a superincumbent mass; weight they got, no doubt, but without strength, action, or spirit. For in these instances, as in all others, where there is a sudden attempt made in breeding; as to size, the effort will be found to end in a colt or filly made without a due proportion of parts, and, therefore, more or less awkward or unwieldy. If our Government was fully instructed as to the unsettled, indiscriminate, and fatal system—or no system rather—that prevails amongst the Irish farmers who so largely breed horses that enter the ranks of our cavalry; and would investigate this subject through the ample means of information open to it, I think the silent but forcible monitors of facts and figures upon the character and standard of supply now, as compared with the past, would be productive, of necessity, of the happiest results. The leaders and law-givers of England are far too prescient and wise to ignore from any cause a great national shame and grievance, calling for the promptest attention and reform. This recent great war on the continent having most fortunately for the future interests of horse-breeding and of the English cavalry opened up a means of absorption for those defective mares that have since the introduction of a new proprietary in Ireland been too largely scattered through the island, bearing a most objectionable "bar sinister;" the *apropos* opportunity should not be allowed to pass without a warning to England not to let slip the time for a national effort at regeneration of our general horses at a period that the accident of circumstances and the operations arising therefrom have most fortunately left open for utilization. This indiscriminate mating of unsuitable "crosses" and unguided or ungoverned operations in breeding by Irish farmers must, somehow, be altered, or, the too patent sad causes resulting from pursuance of the system must too surely be endured in the hour of need and trial, should such ever arrive. A mode, plain, simple, and effective, must be adopted to place within public reach the only true and reliable means of improvement—*carefully and judiciously selected stallions.* As all the native Irish mares have got a sufficient infusion of good blood in their veins, to render a few years persistence in this course productive of even greater results than those which have, from a similar system adopted on the continent, at present left the English markets mainly dependent upon the importation of Prussian, Hungarian, Russian, and other foreign animals, for the supply of high-class harness and riding horses, improved character of produce would result, and command higher prices, affording the best premium that can be offered a community to "go and do likewise." It has been stated that beef-growing in Ireland was superseding the old *penchant* for horse-breeding. I think I can show that any falling off in the numerical supply from that country proceeds from a different cause or causes. No! Paddy is no beef-grower from choice. He'd sooner see his four-year-old colt figure prominently in the local farmers' steeplechase, or jump the "Pound Wall" at Ballin-a-sloe fair, and be greeted by the wild, mad, exultant cheer of his admiring fellows than carry away ten times over the brightest award that successful competition places at the disposal of the cattle feeder.

I have undertaken to make an effort to show that the numerical decrease in Ireland's horse supply of late years did not proceed, as has been somewhere by a recent writer suggested, from a partiality on behalf of the native Irish for beef-growing, consequent on increased high prices in that commodity. Possibly statistics or other pertinent modes of investigation would offer a *prima facie* case, at present in support of such a theory; but, I think, a shallow dip beneath the surface will fix the changes in those matters of decreased horse supply and advanced beef raising in Ireland to the consequences brought about from the inexorable necessities attendant upon comparatively recent legislative enactments and contingent changes, rather than from any deficiency of taste in horsebreeding or want of faith in returns therefrom.

Within the last quarter of a century, not only has the entire aspect of the most fertile portions of Ireland undergone a singularly beneficial change, but also much of the rough and waste lands that afforded good horse pasturage have, under the reclamatory influence of draining and subsoiling, become rich pastures, suited to the occupation, tastes, and habits of the English and Scotch settlers of recent advent, whom the operations of the "Incumbered Estates Act" brought amongst us, owners and workers of Irish land.

For a period extending far into the past, up to about the last twenty years, a vast expanse of agricultural area of acres in Ireland was mapped and plotted out into an infinity of small "holdings." They varied from the cottier's "half acre of garden" to the "strong farmer's" homestead, with its appanage of from fifty acres upwards. But the majority of the land was noted for the disparity of its pasturable fields to those undergoing the culture of the potato and cereal growing population.

Like all lands remarkable for fecundity, the dwellers on the soil were characterised by a much less beneficial and desirable style of agricultural economy than that which marks the operations of the inhabitants in more sterile lands. The natives of Scotland form an example of this theory, as do those of Italy, Greece, and Ireland. Where "Mother Nature" is most prolific and bountiful, there will be found unsystematic and improvident sons of toil.

The uneconomic and wasteful system of very small fields—originated as the necessity of farming operations upon a minute scale by a numerous and poor agricultural population—was the first great objection in the disposition of the land that attracted the recent Scotch and English settlers under the disinheriting edict of the court in Henrietta Street, Dublin.

The system pursued to alter the face of things in this respect is well and generally appreciated in Ireland, and is possibly understood in England and elsewhere. The old aristocracy of the kingdom, careless and unfrugal as the wretched retainers under their feudal rule, designated tenants, in painfully rare instances appreciated the objectionable state of their land under such an improvident and helpless dispensation as that within the command of the poor "small farmers," and the very wretched cottier tenants with their "little plot o' land."

The exodus from Ireland at this period, and through the subsequent years of its depopulation, was mainly caused by the improvement system that had for its object the advanced farming code, the application of which, up to the present, has eventuated in substituting oxen and sheep for men and horses, or, in more remarkable terms, *beef* and *mutton* for *soldiers* and "*re-mounts.*" I call attention only to facts, attempted deductions might fail to effect by my pen that which, through reflection of my readers, may be brought about.

The light and superficial husbandry adopted and pursued by the Irish people (I speak generally) up to the time of the extensive confiscation by the hammer of the auctioneer, necessitated large assistance from horse-power. Limestone and "culem" (small coal for burning the stone to lime) had to be drawn, the fields had to be ploughed, harrowed, and rolled, turf had to be drawn from the neighbouring bog, hay, corn, potatoes, and roots carted home in due season. From the agricultural operations upon that scale which were formerly general in Ireland, horse labour was, of necessity, inseparable; whereas, in dealing with big fields and large farms of later growth, steam-power, aided by the labour of heavy imported horses, has preference, and is, of late years, adopted by those who had experienced its value in their own countries, and by those in Ireland who have had the wisdom and opportunity to follow a commendable example.

The native Irish farmers, like the Arabs, were predisposed to the possession of mares; for, while discharging some duty of draught or burthen to her owners, she was, as a rule, either rearing a foal, or "in a fair way to become a mother"—more frequently both. It was thus that a prodigious horse supply from such an area of land, and so poor a population, was formerly derived from Ireland. With the advent of new systems, that necessitated the demolition of little homesteads and small tillage farms, and the expatriation of their ruined inmates under "the arrangement system," that afforded the means of transport to America, or the more stern and cruel operations of eviction by the Sheriff and his myrmidons, came two great blows to the thews and sinews of Old England in time of war—loss of men, who made, at least, brave soldiers, and with them the necessity and opportunity that kept her cavalry and artillery "remount" supply in that state of efficiency that drew forth the envy and encomiums of civilized Europe. May not we, therefore, infer that the falling off in the number of horses produced in Ireland, and the increased supply of beef from that country, is a state of things derivable from the change in affairs I have endeavoured to depict, rather than from a preference for beef producing, as the more remunerative of the two. It is obvious that cattle feeding becomes a necessity of large pasturable tracts of land; as horse labour is of small agricultural, or tillage, farms, and that, where on the former a comparatively unemployed, or wholly idle lot of mares, could not be calculated upon to pay so steady and safe a return as beef, still, in the latter kind of farming, where the mares' work goes against expenses of their keep, and where the character of the farms was not commensurate with cattle raising, the Irish horse breeder was urged into a congenial, and, under his peculiar circumstances, remunerative system of horse breeding, for which, however, so great an opportunity no longer exists. The fewer horses, and more extended beef supply, from Ireland, is simply consequent upon an altered state of rural economy there, brought about by Acts of the Legislature of England in recent years, and not upon any want of a continuance of the native taste for horse breeding, or faith in its remunerative results.

Let the Irish, even yet, be only directed through their poverty and scrupulous economy in such matters, to the adoption of reasonably supplied government stallions, from which a desirable progeny may naturally be anticipated, and England will need not expensive government studs for her military requirements, provided some efficient steps are taken for securing to the Government the offspring of their own outlay and exertions, which the present unpenalized state of export in horses, and the facilities for competition offered foreigners, is entirely opposed to. Our Continental neighbours cannot grumble, as in all cases of emergency affecting horse supply abroad, means are resorted to, to prevent and cripple exportation as much as possible, where it is not entirely interdicted.

CHAPTER VII.

THE observations, with which I close the foregoing remarks, must be taken to mean that though the native taste for horse breeding in Ireland would be fostered and stimulated to a great extent by the promising and encouraging hopes that a cheap and facile use of desirable sires would give; nevertheless the changes to which I have pointed in the rural economy of that land, will now largely operate to render numerical returns in horse supply painfully less, at the same time that the quality will be largely improved.

With very prose facts staring the country in the face, that no logic or sophistry can soundly argue, or fallaciously reason away, regarding our alarming position, and when it has been proved by practical results amongst the great military nations of Europe that Government supervision has been a success where tried, it then no longer becomes a question of *principle*, but *of coin*.

It appears from the report of the "Select Committee," appointed upon Lord Rosebery's motion in the House of Lords, by which it was hoped not only to find out evils but to suggest a remedy for them if discovered, that they did not take into their consideration the influence had upon general horses from which our re-mounts are derived, by the present system of "short-cut" racing with flying cripples, splendid "roarers," and immature youngsters. Nor did they deal in any practical way with the cavalry supply question, considering the subject—as under existing circumstances it is—merged in the larger one of the general horse supply of these kingdoms. Their not having done so would, at any rate, have had no material effect; for it is patent to the public that the source from which we can alone expect to derive the progenitors of our general horse supply in excellence, has, by a stimulus of quite a foreign kind to the utilitarian efforts of the general breeders, and from influences that preponderate in the minds of the majority of those who now sustain *the turf*, improved and maintained the thoroughbred horse. What the aims and ends of those who have done and continue to do this has nothing to do with the present enquiry. The fact remains to us, that at no previous period of the horse's history in these kingdoms has our thoroughbred been so *grand*. BLAIR ATHOL (sold for over 12,000 guineas to an English stud), and FAVONIUS, another Derby winner, we may assert, without fear of contradiction, are as finely modelled horses and as good performers as can be desired. But these are "the plums of the pudding," as are likewise the numerous stallions offered for the favours of high-bred stud matrons. Such horses, or their class, are far removed from the channel in which their individual services would benefit the general breeder; and he is thrown back upon, too often, the "cheap and nasty."

The Great Dictator of the Turf, as the Honourable Admiral Rous has been long dubbed, to a devotion of a lifetime to everything that could impart improvement and stability to the great institution over which he has long exercised so efficient and popular a sway, adds in his dispensations, the exercise of an intellect singularly keen and more than ordinarily well-cultured, in even that patrician order to which he belongs. Upon the subject of THE ENGLISH RACEHORSE where can we look for a better or more thoroughly practical opinion. His edicts on that particular branch of our subject will have the weight and respect they merit from all students of our present difficulty in *equine* affairs, but must be taken *cum grano salis* in certain particulars where the gallant gentleman allows enthusiasm for a sport and system, of which he is the putative parent, to run away with common sense. He writes:—

"My belief is that the present English Racehorse is as much superior to the racehorse of 1750 as he was to the first cross from ARABS and BARBS with English mares; and, again, as they were to the old English racing hack of 1650. The 'form' of FLYING CHILDERS might now win a £30 plate, 'winner to be sold for £40.' HIGHFLYER and ECLIPSE might pull through in a £50 plate, 'winner to be sold for £200.' This may be a strong opinion, but it is founded on the fact that whereas 150 years ago the Eastern horses and their first 'cross' were the best and fastest in England, at this day a second-class racehorse can give five stone to the best ARABIAN or BARB, and beat them from one to twenty miles. I presume, therefore, that the superiority of the English horse has improved in that ratio above the original stock."

Such are "the Admiral's" own words; and as far as the pace, weight-carrying ability, and staying powers of the best type of the modern racer are treated in his remarks, there is nothing of sophistry, and his assumed facts can only, with justice, be regarded as a fair analogical deduction from the incontestable premises he adduces.

Before Lord Rosebery's Committee, on the 19th of May, 1873, we have Admiral Rous, saying:—

"The stature of thoroughbred stock has increased since the year 1700 an inch every 25 years, and whereas the average size of horses then was 13 hands 3 inches, the average is now 15 hands 2 inches, and they can carry twice as much weight as 100 years ago. Our English thorough-bred horses are the best in the world. There is nothing equal to them, as long as a thorough-bred horse can give five or six stone to an Arab, I do not care what the Arab is."

This is all very well, but we can never forget that the first step in the rising of the ladder to the proud pre-eminence which the English blood horse, and those of other countries, derived from him, hold in every arena of sport, fashion, or war, is remotely due to our Eastern importations of Arab and Barb. Though this is admitted on all hands, the idea of again having recourse to the sons of the desert as harem lords is by no means generally popular; and so far as the primary consideration of the male in reproduction goes, the Englishman and his fellow Britons having brought their own horse to the highest state of perfection and ascendancy as illustrated in the sound short-legged class of race horse that we find to-day, not by any means so scarce as biased detractors of the turf are bitterly prone to urge. We naturally look upon the perfect horse of these islands as the improvement upon the improver in our horse stock, and the *summum bonum* of all that is excellent in his kind, and will not adopt the theories so ably and logically urged in favour of the great-hearted, hardy, and indomitable aristocrat of the desert. Indomitable under the conditions to which the climatic and other influences in his sphere of action submit him. Nor need we do so, whether it is a desirable move or not towards effecting the maintenance of our horses up to their present standard. Let us take care only that the breeders of our general and re-mount horses are not necessarily compelled to supply us from polluted, objectionable, and degenerating sources at home. Be careful that they are afforded the best seed for producing a sound and desirable crop. At present the vast majority of country sires, standing at prices such as breeders of general horses would pay, are the mere offscourings of the racing stables—animals too inferior to be entrusted with the propagation of youngsters upon which large private interests would be staked; but, alas! deemed eligible for the production of stock, on the supply of which, in purity and excellence, the strength of our country may at an unknown, but possible period, depend largely.

So long as the choice of stallions remains free to caprice, parsimony, or want in judgment in private individuals, there can be no such guarantee of a derivative benefit as that which would be insured by the laws of nature, if, by a wise legislative enactment, the duty of providing in high excellence the sires of the country either devolved upon the Government, or, as a modification of interference, that it was enacted that no stallion should be maintained for re-productive purposes unlicensed by Government. We may assume that men fully competent would be appointed to the arduous posts of inspection of districts, and that no local feeling or influence, or mere mercenary motives would be allowed to govern their judgment. Until some such wise economy is indulged, we never can be assured that the defective stallions expelled from the turf from being unsound will not, in accordance with the inexorable law of "like begets like," go on, year by year, sowing deeper and wider the most potent means of degeneracy in form, action, constitutional and physical power throughout our general horses.

Blood is desirable and necessary in our stallions; but shapes and action are two great essentials; choose these with good bone, and special attention to wind, eyes, and feet; and having regard to the natural laws that regulate such matters, we shall as undoubtedly derive the happy results of our forethought and reasonable action, as that from a pure source will flow a clear and wholesome stream; and, *vice versa.*

It is admitted that we require some amendment in the system that now supervenes amongst breeders of our general horses. Nobody denies this, that is capable of forming a practical opinion upon the subject; and, therefore, we may rely upon it that horse-loving England will never allow a canker such as this to eat its way into the very core of her physical strength.

There is a danger that legislative enactment, perfectly reasonable and imperative, regarding the general horse stock of these kingdoms, would lose its popularity, and become quite obnoxious, if it attempted anything like a sweeping and coercive turf reform. And as the turf can, by selection, supply for years to come the sound and beautiful general stock horses that the country will need, I had almost made up my mind to avoid allusion to subjects, the discussion of which is impatiently endured and petulantly assailed, in quarters where personal partial feeling is allowed to over-ride the consideration of public weal.

That the English turf has risen to its present importance, as a national institution, under the ægis of a utilitarian aim, having for its object the improvement of the general horse stock, is an axiomatic assertion. Let us glance, then, at how it has performed its mission, by what means improvement was attained, and what are the existing defects of the system, that are supposed to re-act in an inverse ratio to that, from the operation of which we have arrived at a very great state of improvement in our stock.

All my individual sympathies are with *the turf*; I am an *habitué* of its various arenas for more than a quarter of a century; and, if all this world could afford mortal, was placed at my disposal, I must in truth say, if the opportunity of paying my humble share of devotion to our great Isthmean Idol was withheld, I should not be anything like content. Therefore, it may be assumed that what I may write hostile to its operations, is produced entirely from a sense of public duty, and an affectionate and conscientious belief, that in using the knife it is only in the earnest hope that the operation may tend to lead to a wholesome cure.

A nebulistic assertion in a recent letter of Admiral Rous, where danger, from no given cause, to the prospects of the turf is announced, is an admission of internal decay, or general deteriorating action, very painfully suggestive to all well-wishers to "the national pastime."

We may, from authentic records and traditionary assertion assume that, though at no time in turf history were there such fine specimens of good and grand thoroughbreds; neither used there to be, some years back, anything like the vast numbers of unsound racehorses—wretched abortions, and spindle-shanked deformities—as may be now seen in the training stables of the country.

Can we, if we are rational beings, for one moment fail to deduce from given and patent facts, the perfect solution to this state of things. Let us regard the past aspect of affairs, and the introduction of a new era, that made its advent with that deplorable system of handicapping, from which, and short-cut racing, we may be enabled to show the present lamentable want of soundness and stoutness may be traced.

Nearly everybody knows that the traditions of the turf, and the annals of Weatherby convey to us the assurance of more bone, power, and stamina in thoroughbreds during the *regime* of the ancient system of severe contests, and weight for age, penalties and allowances, over severe courses, than we can now, in a general way, find. It is obvious that under such conditions it would be quite useless to maintain in training anything not able to compete on comparatively equal terms with its opponents under heavy weights, and cruelly severe ordeals of long distance heats. The obvious induction is, that if the intensity of the operations was severe, the integrity of the original object of the turf was maintained. That object being the propagation and culture of the sound and stout. But all that were bred and trained were not of this calibre, and consequently useless for racing under the then existing system. This state of things kept the ownership of race horses in the hands of noblemen and gentlemen of mark and merit in the land. They did not regard the sport and the sustainment of their studs in a commercial or grovelling pecuniary spirit. They raced because men in their position raced, and because they felt in supporting the turf they were abetting one of our greatest national bulwarks. Under this system there were no complaints of want of bone, weight-carrying power, and stamina, in the thoroughbred stallions who, after their turf career, began to exercise the offices of sires through country districts for the begetting of general and military horses. Those of their fellows that were too slow for racing, being fine-grown strong horses, were subjected to emasculation and drafted to some of the purposes of saddle or harness work; so that, an operation which now the weedy and weakly off-casts of the turf are not thought worth, in former days and with a more useful class of animal reduced the number of thoroughbred stallions down to a narrower and more select compass than in our day.

The creation of handicapping was a fell blow, at any rate, to that object for which the government, or monarch, had subscribed Royal Plates—inducement to breed horses the best calculated to carry weight and stay over courses of exceptional severity. Handicapping in its object, was, perhaps, as perfect a means of negativing this intention as ingenuity and experience could devise. It may be desirable to explain that by the term "handicapping" is meant a system of estimating and penalizing the capacity of race horses according to their relative ages and performances, and by a distribution, by an authority styled a handicapper, of different weights according to the assumed ability to race of each intending competitor; giving the *worst* as well as the best a chance of winning. It is supererogatory to add, that, in view of such an innovation many " weeds " and " wastrels " were fostered and preserved from their speed for long or short distances under light weights, that would have no chance in the old style of racing, as above described. This then was "the beginning of the end." For one fine-grown, sound, weight-carrying and long-running race-horse to be found to-day, an abominably great number of unsound, " weedy," half-milers, or four-furlong shadows can be polled. The fact is, our needs in any great popular undertaking beget our required instruments. Handicapping required bad horses to sustain its purpose, and that we have them now is sufficiently illustrated by the very table of entries for the handicap races of this Spring (1874). The five great handicap races of the Spring and early Summer are the THE GREAT NORTHAMPTONSHIRE STAKES, the NEWMARKET HANDICAP, the CITY AND SUBURBAN, the METROPOLITAN, and the CHESTER CUP. For these important events, over sufficiently long courses to test the staying powers of any race horse, there is a suggestive deficiency in the numerical entries when compared with a *short distance* handicap at Lincoln—*one mile*—of an earlier date for decision than any of them. *That* got one hundred and fifty-nine entries, while the Chester Cup—a race of great popularity with the public—has got no more than eighty intending competitors for its *two miles and two furlongs essay*. And we may draw more food for contemplation from the recorded facts that we never have, in our day, the same strong entries for long distance handicaps that we have for short ones; avowedly from the great scarcity of race-horses capable of successfully covering a long distance course. If we have a few such horses contending in such races, what happens them? Their superior merit brings them to the front, which causes them to be penalized with weight in some subsequent contest, sufficient to have victory snatched from them by some miserable "plating" cripple. "We cannot gather grapes of thorns, or figs of thistles!" Neither can we expect the sound and stout race-horse to be propagated as the rule, not the exception, from such means.

Admiral Rous, in writing upon the subject we have under consideration, has evidenced the performances of steeple-chase horses in the present day as exemplifying the solidity of his anti-degeneracy theory. "The Admiral" is so fond of seizing upon singular examples to bolster up his untenable generalities, that, I think, independent of a wish not to appear personally hostile in my writing to one so deservedly liked and respected, I can give strong support to my antagonistic opinions, by wielding, through the facile means of a long quotation, a more trenchant force than any individual opinion could bring to bear. In an admirable article from the *Field* newspaper of Saturday, March 14, 1874, we read the following:—

"Noticeably enough, at just about the very same time when the gentlemen sportsmen were protesting in the Vale last week against the Grand National Hunt line as being too big and stiff, the Grand National Hunt Committee was issuing a protest on its own account. The owners or managers of horses at Aylesbury would not run because they considered the country to be dangerously strong, whereas the committee considers the country as too often adopted now-a-days to be dangerously weak; 'the manner in which lessees of courses have lowered and cut down fences during the last few seasons is most detrimental to steeple-chasing;' and, again, the committee begs to suggest that lessees 'keep up the fences to a proper standard, as they used to be some years ago, and have the hurdles in the straight run planted firmly in the ground, so as not to fly in every direction when struck.' The committee would further recommend the abolition of 'trappy and unfair fences;' precisely as, at Aylesbury, Lord Queensberry and Lord Charles Ker spoke against 'the trimmed fences' which the local committee had been fashioning. Of course a very material question at once arises here. Has the Grand National Hunt Committee really any powers; or, more pertinently still, have the stewards of meetings anything to do with the management of the meetings to which they give their countenance? It will be observed that the Grand National Hunt Committee only 'expresses an opinion' or 'offers a suggestion' to the lessees of the Liverpool Grand National Steeplechase; whilst some of the best qualified of the stewards at Aylesbury also only 'suggest' to the local committee. Now it is very apparent that, beyond any great men of the country side, or the little men more handy to the town, the stewards are selected mainly for their experience and authority as sportsmen; whereas lessees, clerks of courses, secretaries, and so forth, are or were engaged to carry out the business of the occasion under the direction of their superiors. When Lord George Bentinck put in force his reforms, he did so, caring no more for clerks or secretaries than he did for his own jockey boys. Since then, no doubt, the position has somewhat changed, as many of the officials are now—and we say so much with no intentional disrespect—merely men of business and nothing more. Their undisguised aim is to get together large fields and large companies; and so long as they can achieve success in this way, they care little for the character of the meeting as an exposition of national sport.

"After strolling down through the well-known old town, there was something harsh and grating in being pulled up short for the 'one shilling' head money, as if one were about to witness a cockney scramble rather than a workmanlike set-to over the glorious Vale of our earlier days. We have galloped *pari passu* with the horses as the chase was run, or taken up our point of sight on the hill-side, without being bothered for a shilling, or pestered to back something, or to say if the favourite is 'spinning this journey.' Manifestly, the means for securing large fields and large companies, heavy betting or rows of list men, are the same. Handicaps and light weights have been detrimental alike to the chase and the turf; and we may date this decline over a country to the time when the Liverpool Grand National was transformed from an honest, fair hunting country, at fair hunting weights of 12st. each, into a handicap, since which time no horse carrying 12st. has ever won the Grand National. On the contrary, there have often, year by year, been animals, neither racehorses nor hunters, winning the great cross-country event of the season at 9st. 12lb., 9st. 8lb., 9st. 6lb., 9st. 10lb., 9st. 7lb., 9st. 10lb., and 9st. 12lb. Green, who died only the other day, won the Grand National twice, once at 9st. 12lb. and again at 9st. 7lb.; and lads from the racing stables, on cast-off platers, have had quite their turn over Liverpool. Now it necessarily follows that light weights must make light fences. A weed with a racing weight on his back could never force his way through an unshorn bullfinch, and so the fences have to be 'trimmed,' and the hurdles to give and 'fly in every direction' like the sham jumps at Islington, so that the pumped-out daisy-cutters may be able to gallop through them. Riding a steeplechase over a fair hunting country should be very much like riding to hounds; and 'Nimrod' long since said in one of his letters that which we may say again here: 'There is a description of persons who are generally defeated when business is to be done, and those are your very light weights. In my experience of foxhunting I have observed that men above eleven stone for the most part beat men under eleven stone, and for this reason: the very light man says, '"Anything will carry me,"' and if he hears of a slight bit of blood which no man of any size will buy because he can't carry weight, he goes and purchases him. The consequence of this is, as force must be opposed to force, the little horse and his rider are knocked backwards and thrown over by fences which a heavier man on a heavier horse would break through if he could not clear.' Precisely so ; and as the light weight would not accept if there were fences which would knock him backwards, we provide hurdles which will give, and trappy and trim fences over which men are killed, while the giants of old 'lived' over far bigger countries. These small fences, say the committee, 'are the cause of nearly all the accidents ; and by having good fair upstanding hunting fences the pace would be much reduced, thereby rendering falls far less frequent and severe.' But the committee must do something more than suggest; and, as they have already enacted that the minimum weight in a steeplechase handicap shall be 10st., they must go on and raise the strength of the line in proportion, so as to bring us back to fair hunting weights over a fair hunting country. Still, on the face of it, there is something absurd in a steeplechase handicap—at least, as at present arrived at by performances. A faint-hearted weed may be got over Liverpool, but be useless over a stronger country ; and we may point this by the Aylesbury National, where, in the open handicap, Daybreak received nearly a stone from Judge and nearly two stone from Ryshworth, and he beat them by miles—one being a great favourite for Liverpool at the time. But Daybreak looked more like carrying a man, and was, moreover, a fine fencer ; while the line was a fair hunting country, which he went over without a lead and without a mistake, with the other two floundering at almost every fence they came to."

Well done, independent *Field !* the "Gentleman's" paper. This is "scotching the viper" and no mistake. It has been long apparent to others, as well as to the late Earl of Derby, that the speculative order of race and steeplechase meetings was the very worst creation, for the sustainment in its integrity of the orthodox mission of the Turf, that ever had existence. The self-evident object of the promoters of such meetings is individual aggrandisement : and although the *regime* of such men as Mr. Warner, and the Messrs. Verral, leave nothing to be cavilled at so far as their own integrity and ability is concerned, it is, unhappily, axiomatically true that the system and its contingencies for which they cater have too much of the miserable plating business about them to afford encouragement to the sustenance of that class of animal the Turf was inaugurated to foster and maintain; but, upon the contrary, opens up a channel for emolument to the owners of miserable quadrupeds, fit for nothing else but scrambling in such an arena.

No author having the subject before us at heart, ought to glance at the probable effect of steeplechasing proper upon the production of desirable horses, without, at least, paying his humble meed of praise to KILDARE HUNT STEEPLE CHASE MEETING — better known as PUNCHESTOWN — so largely indebted to that thorough practical expert, the present Earl of Howth, more familiar in conjunction with this great institution as VISCOUNT ST. LAWRENCE. Here may be seen a line of big, fair hunting country unequalled in the world, and a munificence in prizes and completeness of arrangement beyond all praise. And, just look at the consequence—except that you may, rarely, see a "weedy blood" in the "Light Weight Military," the general competitors are remarkable for those qualities which can alone insure victory in such an ordeal, viz., blood, size, bone, and stoutness. Here is an example worthy to be followed. Here we have the happy results of salutary effects from judicious cause.

I have before said that at the present day we have examples of the highest quality and excellence in some of the stallions who, at heavy prices for their favours, are reserved for the Belgravian mothers of our *pur sang* horses. But their very excellence negatives to the country the immediate benefit to be derived from their service at the stud. And the desire to breed *mainly for speed* now-a-days causes to be kept for the purpose of brood-mares many mis-shapen "flyers," that, although they may transmit their pace to posterity, are not calculated to impart any of those essential points and desirable characteristics that we want as the foundation for our military and general horses.

Can we wonder, then, that a well-known sporting writer, when descanting on the handicap entries the other day, should *naively* write regarding the paucity of competitors for the longer courses, that, "*long races are not so popular as they used to be, owing to the difficulty of getting horses to stay the distance.*" Alas! verily, the means cannot *justify*, though they have *accomplished* the end. It is surely a bad day for the encouragement to breed sound and stout, and for those that look beneath the surface and into the future, when they contemplate the unpromising position that £1,000 is added to a short cut handicap in the month of March, and that young blood ones are tried before Christmas. In other words, when, possibly, only ten months old, or less; and certainly not more than eleven months and some days old.

Another phase in this consideration is the multitude of minor race meetings that have sprung up all over the country, affording an inferior class of race-horse, known, technically, as "platers," sustenance and encouragement. It is well-known what a staunch patron of the turf in its integrity the late Earl Derby was, and how eminently capable of enunciating utilitarian maxims, and propounding sound and far-sighted views concerning any subject he devoted the exercise of his truly great and highly cultivated intelligence to. In the last letter that has been published, and which his Lordship gave the world, on the subject of racing, he says, in forcible and monitory language, " I know that some persons consider the multiplication of races and starters as a sign of the turf's success. I look on them as the very opposite, and I should hail with satisfaction the disappearance from the Calendar of one half of the present meetings. I take it that the deterioration of the turf in public estimation, of which there is no doubt, is mainly owing to the fact that the majority of horses are now in the possession of men who run for profit and not for sport, who care nothing for the animal, who cannot afford to wait for a return of their money, and in whose hands a wretched animal, especially if not quite so wretched as he is thought" (handicap morality!), "is as valuable as one of high class" (a premium on deterioration!), "if not more so. Now, this vicious system is mainly fostered, first, by *premature running of two-year-olds*" (the italics are not his Lordship's); secondly, by the multiplication of short races, which enables horses to be brought out oftener, and thus to afford more frequent opportunities of gambling; thirdly, by the great preponderance of handicaps."

These are wise words of a great statesman and thorough sportsman, who was a true votary of racing; and who, in this his last public essay upon the sport and institution he loved, leaves these *a fortiori* views to his survivors for contemplation, as sound in policy as they are true in inference, and unanswerable in argument.

Figures are dry but powerful illustrations. In 1873 the number of horses entered for the five spring handicaps above named were 400; in 1874 the aggregate amounts to 75 less. The average number of racehorses in training, between 1860 and 1870, was 2,400; but at present (1874) the revised returns give a total of 1,665. If 200 for Scotland and Ireland be added, which is, probably, an estimate in excess of the actual number, it remains that there were nearly 600 more horses in training six years past than there are now. And this at a time when England's wealth was never so great, nor her people more disposed to and capable of indulging in their favourite enjoyment.

I think it may be said without offence to anyone, or disparaging of anything, that the sooner the standard of our racing studs are numerically and physically improved the better! And the more rapidly will the objectionable, regarding the horses, vanish. But how is this to be practically aided towards consummation?

We find, from history, tradition, and living evidence, in the establishment of Royal Plates in the past, when the turfites, through their institution, were offered a stimulus not afforded by opportunities and rewards of our own gambling era, that there was a vastly more general supply of sound animals with stamina. The money for these Royal Plates, with a view to encourage the propagation of blood horses of a superior type, when race-horses were not numerous, and the prizes awaiting their successful efforts moderate, was all fair, legitimate, and desirable; but the sums now expended for Queen's plates could be, almost anyhow, better applied for advancement of the object they were instituted to promote and maintain. And this, too, without interfering to any appreciable extent with racing and its votaries. The Turf has, within its own system, ample prizes *now* to induce to the production of as high class horses as the materials for their propagation will allow, irrespective of any consideration the Royal Donations might evoke, as these gifts have of late years completely failed in inducing the competition and contests which they were inaugurated to engender, and in former times produced! Surely the Master of the Horse should be called upon to give some consideration to this subject, of a more general character than condensing three of the Royal Plates in one at Newmarket, as recently announced in sporting organs; and having a regard to the time-honoured adage of "new brooms," the present is an opportune period.

The turf men, in simple justice, have no right or reason

to expect the continuance of a national grant, such as royal plates, where the system they adopt and have created to further private ends conduces to the consummation of results at variance with, and non-conformal to the objects that originally instituted such donations to the turf; for it is generally conceded, even by those who rush into untenable and intemperate assumptions and generalities in support of an effete and degenerating *regime*, that the royal plates fail altogether in bringing to the post now such fields and such horses as in the days of their novitiate marked the practical utility of their operation.

It is maintained that the early racing of immature blood horses has mainly contributed to defeat the object of those time-honoured grants. For the inducements to find out the racing merits of *thorough-bred foals* is under the present order of things too cogent and ample to hope for the sustenance of grand youngsters, until more advanced age and indurated muscles might have a greater chance of withstanding the terrible rigours of the training stable.

It is argued with pecuniary force that the sum of £2 10s. a week for each race-horse's training is a considerable item, and that, if breeders and owners of youngsters don't apply themselves to secure some of the prizes awarded to successful juvenile competitors they can only hope for immense monetary outlay and great loss. Well, doubtless, this is so. But what does it suggest? Simply, that, although the turf left to its own operations, unimpeded by Governmental interference, may, under its present code of operations, entirely fail to supply the country generally with the *sound* and *stout* horses of former days, its internal interests are of sufficient magnitude to induce its votaries to produce occasionally the finest specimens of the English blood horse. So long as fine thorough-bred stallions can be found, and these it is clear the English turf will continue to produce

—the influence of the stallion being calculated in the breeding of general horses as one hundred times greater than the mare, for he may get one hundred foals, while a mare, as a rule, only produces one—I think we may say that the only thing we require in addition is to take care that the *meres* for our war and general horses are left in sufficient character and quantity in these kingdoms.

I intend here to call the reader's attention to notices from *The Times*, which I annex, and which speak trumpet-tongued as to the sad state of things into which we have drifted regarding the *equine* strength of the country, and from which it is so necessary and absolutely imperative that we should be released.

The first thing to discover in its naked deformity to the eye of the public and the legislature is this great festering sore in the heart of the nation; and having clearly exhibited this objectionable and melancholy fact to exist beyond hope of controversion or doubt, proceed to look for the remedy, cure, and eventual abolition of the corroding and debilitating evil.

"Lord Rosebery's Commission," under royal warrant, has elicited facts that, being officially vouched, give all the *ægis* of high authority to the pen that reproduces in support of its labours salient points, elicited from the efforts of the committee. At least, this is my individual opinion. And be this my apology for the following lengthy extracts. The first is from *The Times*, 15th August, 1873.

THE SUPPLY OF HORSES.

We have before us, in a Blue-book of 350 pages, the result of the Committee appointed on Lord Rosebery's motion to inquire into the alleged deterioration of the breed of horses in Great Britain. Thirty-nine witnesses were examined during a period extending from the 10th of March to the 16th of June, and the result may be best summed up in the concluding paragraph of the Report, in which the Committee trust that by "the collection of evidence and by the attention they have called to the subject, they have contributed somewhat to the objects for which they were appointed."

It was hardly, indeed, from the first supposed that any actual or immediate good would result from this inquiry. "In this country," says the Report, "Government interference in such matters is justly unpopular even when practicable." The formation of Government military studs has been tried and abandoned in France. The system for some time past employed in India has been subject to many and grave objections, and we cannot certainly refrain at least from doubts as to a management which could reject as unsound, worthless, or worn-out, horses approved by General Peel, and passed by the Veterinary College.* The remedies which, in the opinion of the Committee, are most practicable for this alleged scarcity of horses—a scarcity which, though undoubtedly somewhat exaggerated,† does as undoubtedly exist among certain classes, especially among draught‡ horses and roadsters—are "that the Government should give or add to prizes at Agricultural Shows for Stallions passed sound, which have covered a number of mares at a certain low price in particular districts;" that "any tax operating as a discouragement on a farmer's keeping horses, whether broken or not, should be either at once abolished or considerably modified, while the dealer's license, which, not existing in Ireland, only produces £19,175 here, should be altogether repealed;" and lastly, that the system of warranty should be done away with."

Though they have declined to enter into the vexed question of Army remounts, which they considered, and wisely, as one solely for the military authorities, it must be confessed that some of the evidence given on this important point was startling.

From Mr. Phillips, of Willesden, the Army contractor, we learn that since the Crimean war only one of our Cavalry

---

* Quite possible for horses to be sound and good performers, and worse than worthless as sires for remounts.
  † It is not!!! ‡ Harness, not "draught" horses.

regiments, the 9th Lancers, has been mounted from England, whereas before that time five or six were so supplied. The horses for the Artillery are, indeed, of English breed, but the Cavalry, with the exception named, are mounted from Ireland. The causes of this are, in Mr. Phillips' opinion, and in that of his partner, Mr. East, the change in the regulation age from three to four years old. "The mischief," says Mr. East, "is this:—

"We left off buying three-year-olds for the Army after the Crimean War. We bought three-year-olds for 25 guineas before the Crimean War, then we certainly had not many; their numbers were few, but the quality of them was very good indeed. The Crimean War came, and it was no use attempting to buy young ones; we had to buy older horses about London, and wherever we could, for £40 a piece; and when the war was over they would not go back to the three-year-olds, but would insist upon having four-year-olds, and they gave £50 for them. If I am obliged to pay £15 for keeping my colt for a year, I think it was a hard case for the Government to ask of a farmer to sell them a four-year-old horse for about £3 10s. more than they gave before; because they gave 25 guineas for a three-year-old, and then they asked to have a four-year-old at £30; and when you wanted him kept till he was four years old, you were placed somewhere in the same position as I should be with my colt. You could not have the four-year-old when he was a four-year-old, the foreigner would buy him; the foreigner steps into the market, and then the farmers can get £40 for him; but if you had bought the horse at three years old, he would not have got into the foreigner's hands."

This statement Mr. Phillips, who "mounts the whole of the Artillery in England," corroborates, and further gives us the following piece of by no means satisfactory information:—

"263. Supposing that there was any sudden call for horses within two or three months, how soon could you get 2,000 or 3,000 together?—I should be put to my wits' end to do it.
"264. Will it or will it not be an affair of price?—No, it is not a question of money; it is a question of not having the animals.
"265. You actually think that there are not the animals on sale in England to provide 2,000 or 3,000 horses for the Artillery at a sudden emergency?—Certainly not, in England. I firmly believe that at the present time every farmer in England who farms over 200 acres of land is short-handed with his horses."

Nor is Sir Henry Storks much more confident on the subject:—

"1,599. Is it your experience that you could not find 2,000 horses in Great Britain?—I think I could find them if I went with any quantity of money in my pocket, but I could not find them at the regulation price, nor could I find them in a very short period.
"1,600. Should you find any difficulty in procuring the proper number of Cavalry horses to put our Army on a war footing?—I should think that they could not be procured easily, but there are officers here who will give a better opinion upon that subject than I can do."

One of those officers, Major-General Robert Wardlaw, is of opinion that perhaps the number could be found at first, "but whether the supply could be kept up is another question, because we should require to keep increasing the number." This, too, is the opinion of Colonel Price, of the Horse Artillery, and of Colonel Valentine Baker, late of the 10th Hussars. Colonel Jenyns is even more explicit.

"2,017. Have you ever considered at all the question of how we should provide horses in case of a sudden military emergency?—I think that at the present time it would be quite impossible to supply the horses, even if you were to pay £100 or £150 a-piece for them.

"2,018. How many horses would be required to make the Cavalry up to its war footing?—2,464.

"2,019. And how many for the Artillery?—5,000, within a horse or two.

"2,020. With regard to the 5,000 for the Artillery, we have heard already that we should find it almost impossible to get them?—Yes; I think you would find it almost impossible to get them.

"2,021. Is that exclusive of the Train?—Entirely exclusive of the Train. I only allude to the combatant branches.

"2,022. As regards the 2,500, speaking roughly, that you want for the Cavalry, even if you got them within a certain time, they would not be fit for the ranks?—Certainly not.

"2,023. How long does it take to make a horse fit for the ranks?—I consider that a three-year-old horse is not fit for the ranks for a year-and-a-half, owing to his age; it takes that time to get him fit for work and to break him in.

"2,024. And also to his being very much out of condition when bought?—He is certain to be out of condition at three years old.

"2,025. How soon do you think you could buy 2,500 horses if you wanted them? I do not think that on an emergency you would get them now under five or six months.

"2,026. Do you think that you would have to pay £100 a piece for them?—Certainly.

"2,027. That would be an expense on that item alone of £250,000?—Certainly.

"2,028. When you got them they would be horses, and not chargers or trooper horses?—A great many could be made to go in the ranks for fighting purposes, perhaps, in a month; but they would not be broken chargers, or really effective troop horses. I am now alluding to five-year-old horses, horses fit to go on a campaign to-morrow, as far as condition is concerned."

All, therefore, who may with reason be considered as most competent to speak on the subject, are of opinion that there would be a serious difficulty in obtaining in the necessary time the number of horses required to place our Cavalry and Artillery on their proper war footing. What, then, we naturally ask, are the remedies they would suggest? Mr. Phillips at once answers with a suggestion which has struck him, and will perhaps strike others too, as a "practical thing:"—

"348. Do you think that it would answer to have a large establishment of trooper horses, where three years old, or even younger, might be brought and kept until they were four years old?—Yes; but it would cost the Government above £100 a-piece.

"349. Would you not buy them cheaper at three years old than at four years old?—Yes, I believe that that is the only solution of the difficulty. I think that the Government must keep them, for you find that the farmers will not keep them. Things are too dear for them to keep them longer, and you will miss a great many good horses unless you buy them at three years old. A farmer will sell a horse at three years old because it may have a white face, or something for which he does not think it good enough to keep it on longer, and he will take the Government price at that time, but if he does not sell it then, he keeps it on longer, and he gets a better customer for it than the Government at four years old.

"350. Would it not be better for the Government to buy them from the farmers at three years old, and keep them for a year?—I think so.

"351. Do you think that it would be worth while for the Government to buy them at three years old, and keep them either in some general depôt or some depôt for each regiment, until they are four years old?—I think that if you were to increase all your batteries, for instance, 20 per cent., and take three-year-old horses into them, they would mature better. With a battery having 20 extra horses, you have got all the materials there, and you would always come out with your strength and leave 20 horses behind; and every autumn, supposing you want those autumn manœuvres, let every battery colonel send you 20 of his worst horses, and let them go through the autumn manœuvres, and sell them for whatever they will fetch. I think you would not want to create depôts or any extensive establishments, and you would also allow us to begin buying horses on the 1st of April, which we ought to do. That is an idea of my own, and perhaps it is presumptuous of me to say so, but it strikes me as a practical thing."

On the same side follow Lord Vivian, Major Wardlaw, Colonel Price, and Colonel Baker. Colonel Jenyns, while not altogether opposed to the system of purchasing three-year-olds as a reserve fund, thinks the establishment of Government depôts would interfere with the privilege that commanding officers have of purchasing their own horses. To this privilege, on the other hand, Lord Charlemont takes strong objection. Admitting the possibility of Lord Strathnairn's dissent, his Lordship objects altogether to the purchase of horses for the regiments by the Colonels of the regiments. He says:—

"I would have all the horses for army remounts purchased by the Government. I would have all horses for the army service purchased and stationed at proper depôts, to be there conditioned, trained, and broken, and never sent to the regiments till they were fit to go to the ranks.

"622. You object to the system of buying by particular regiments?—Yes, I do. I know that in fairs the colonels of different regiments continually clash against each other in their purchases.

"623. Do you mean that it raises the price?—No, I do not mean in raising the price so much as in interfering with each other's taste or discrimination in the purchase. I think that a great deal of difficulty arises often from the commanding officers of different regiments being in the same fair, and clashing against each other.

"624. Do you mean that their individual tastes clash?—It is not that merely; they want black horses for one regiment, we will say the Life Guards, and the Life Guards want three or four greys for the band. The colonel of the Greys is there, and he is very angry at the greys being taken away from him for the band of the Life Guards."

But Sir Henry Storks does not consider that the purchase of three-year-olds, with a view to keeping them and breaking them to use at four years, is at all an economical arrangement, as "in point of fact the Government would have to pay for the keep of the animal, instead of the breeder, for the additional year." He enforces his point with the following statistics:—

"1,624. Could you give the Committee any information as to the expense of a three-year-old, bought at three and kept till four, of course being used merely for the purpose of breaking up to four years of age?—Yes, I think I could state that. There was a proposal of adding 20 per cent. of three-year-old horses to regiments, and I could state to the Committee exactly what it would cost as regards feeding them, and other incidental expenses. Taking the Cavalry and the Royal Artillery in Great Britain, I have excluded the train of the Royal Engineers, and also the Army Service Corps, but merely taking the Household Brigade, the Cavalry of the Line, and the Artillery, I make it that there are 9,670 horses, and in Ireland, in the Cavalry of the Line, and the Royal Artillery, the number is 3,543 horses. If we add 20 per cent. on the Great Britain establishment, it would make 1,934 horses, and on the Irish establishment it would make 708, giving a total of 2,642 horses. I separate Great Britain from Ireland because the forage is a different price. I make out that the forage of the 1,934 horses in Great Britain would cost £50,001 19s. 2d. a year; and of the 708 in Ireland would cost £15,795 18s. 5d., which makes a total of £65,797 17s. 7d.; and the farriery allowance for 2,645 horses would be £2,009 0s. 5d., making a total of £67,806 18s. That does not include, of course, the cost of the horse, nor the casualties, nor the increased stable accommodation, nor anything like stable implements, such as buckets and things of that sort. Supposing we put the cost price of a three-year-old at £35, his value when four years old would be £60 13s. 4d., and his value when five years old would be £86 6s. 8d.

"There is another question too," he adds, "would have to be considered:—

"Supposing that we had 20 per cent. added to the Cavalry regiments, I have excluded from that calculation anything about an increased establishment as regards those additional horses.
"Which you apprehend would be to a certain extent required?—Yes. The Household Cavalry have 343 men and 275 horses; 20 per cent. would be 55 horses more, so that there would be 330 horses to 343 men. I apprehend that you would scarcely think that would do. Nine regiments of the line have 547 men and 384 horses; adding 20 per cent. would make 778, giving a total of 461 horses to 547 men. Then there are ten regiments of the line that have 417 men and 320 horses; adding 64 for the 20 per cent. would give 384 horses to 417 men. In the Royal Artillery the proportions are also pretty much the same; but I can put that Return in also."

General Peel, in his turn, has a proposal to make, the very opposite of those to which we have hitherto been listening:—

"With regard to the Cavalry, I am afraid I should very much astonish His Royal Highness if I were to say that I should strongly recommend, instead of purchasing horses at four years old, purchasing them at a much earlier age. I think there is a great deal of truth in the old saying that most of the goodness of a horse goes in at his mouth—that is to say, it depends very much upon whether he has been starved or well fed during his youth how he turns out afterwards. However that may be, I am perfectly certain that whatever goodness he has in him will be sooner developed and brought to maturity if he is well fed than if he is starved in the first year or two. If you were to go to Newmarket next December you would be perfectly astonished to see the yearlings that have been recently purchased galloping away there, with heavy weights on their backs, at a good speed; you would hardly know the distinction between them and old horses. Now, I should like to see an experiment of this kind tried; every Colonel of a cavalry regiment should be allowed to purchase a few two-year-olds in October; he would have a far greater number to select from, and pay a smaller price for them than at present. In the October following, if they were well fed in the meantime, you would find that you would be able to put them into the ranks sooner than a four-year-old bought at that time."*

The question of remounting cavalry will, in his opinion, always be one of price. Amid such a mass of conflicting evidence and opinions, who can say that the committee did not do wisely in refraining from the proposal of any "special or detailed scheme for providing army remounts?"

It is, however, satisfactory to know that while no one is willing to dispute the falling off in the quantity of the material at our disposal, that the quality remains the same is equally indisputable.† All the military authorities we have quoted are agreed on this point. It is merely a question of price, they say. The horses are as good as ever, but they are dearer, and there are not so many of them. The same remark, according to Mr. Greene, M.P., a M. F. H., applies equally to hunters. Horses which two years ago he could mount the servants of his hunt upon at an average of £40 apiece, are now hardly to be found at all, and never under £60 or £80. It is the same with roadsters—a class much patronized, according to Mr. Phillips, by foreigners—and with carriage horses; the latter, indeed, says Mr. East, are hardly to be got for any money:—

"If you told me that you would give me £400 for a pair of carriage horses that you dare put your wife behind—a pair of nice, good horses, worth £200—and gave me a fortnight to get them in, I would not guarantee to buy them. I do not think there is a man in London that could do it, or that I could go to a dealer's yard and get a pair of carriage horses, such as you would like to put your wife behind, for £400. At this moment we have now got 300 lying by and not earning a shilling, and we would not do that if we could supply London by going into the market and getting what we want directly; it is only that we may have them by us when we want them in May and June."

Even the number of racehorses chargeable to duty is, according to the returns published up to the 31st of December, 1872, less than it has been in any previous year up to 1866. It was then returned as 2,309, against 2,310 for last year, which shows

---

* The concentration of practical wisdom and common sense in General Peel's remarks here ought to be written in letters of gold, and they derive great additional weight from the consideration of the immense stimulus the prospect of an assured and early market would give to general horse-breeding.

† It is not so; according to the author's individual experience there are more " weeds " and more unsoundness than thirty years ago.

a decrease of 163 against the 2,473 of 1871. Mr. Edmund Tattersall, a name which is a household word among all lovers of horses, also speaks as to the general scarcity, and brings three good names to corroborate what he says:—

> "Judging from all the information that I have received from gentlemen whose opinions I get, there is a great scarcity of a good class of horses bred. I could mention different districts in which I have information from gentlemen who live there—for example, Mr. Thomas Drake. Mr. Challoner Smith, and Mr. Villebois, whom I saw this morning. They all agree upon this point —that where there were fifty good horses bred in their districts twenty years since, you cannot find five of the same sort of horse bred now. Mr. Challoner Smith speaks of a district round Abingdon, where he has lived all his life."*

One only stands out in opposition to this formidable array of alarmists, with the statement that in his judgment

> "There are more horses in the country at this moment than ever there were, and they never were so good, and their stature has increased. The stature of thorough-bred stock has increased since the year 1700 an inch every twenty-five years; and whereas the average size of horses then was 13 hands 3, the average is now 15 hands 2; and in point of carrying power, they can carry twice as much weight as they could a hundred years ago."

Admiral Rous has, as of course all England knows, devoted a considerable portion of his life—thirty years according to his own statement—to the study of racing and racehorses and of horses generally, but he cannot say that he thinks there are as many horses bred in this country as formerly. "With the price of beef and mutton it will not pay to breed horses," he says, "but you can get as many as you want from the Continent." In the event of a war, however, the Admiral would not rely upon foreign horses. "In the event of a war," he says:—†

> "You would lay your hand upon 500,000 in this country, and you would look at all of them and take what you please; if the country is ever threatened, there are 2,000,000 horses in the country, and it would be very hard if you could not get 500,000 to serve you."

On the 16th August, 1873, *The Times* continues:—

THE SUPPLY OF HORSES.

We have seen in our former notice of the Report of this Commission how prevalent was the opinion of the witnesses

---

* Does not this corroborate the Author's views?
† This is fallacious enthusiasm.

examined as to the real existence of a scarcity of horses in this kingdom, and we propose now to glance at the reasons assigned and the remedies suggested for that scarcity. As regards the former, treated by each successive witness at greater or less length, with greater or less degree of detail, they may be comprised, according to the evidence, under these three heads : The higher prices given to our breeders by the foreign buyers; the extraordinary demand made upon our market during the Franco-Prussian war; and the fact that the farmers find it pays them better now to breed sheep and oxen than to breed horses :—*

"Chairman.—Do you attribute this rise in the prices only to the general rise in the price of other commodities?—I think that although it has paid the farmer very well to breed horses at the price that he has had, the price that he gets now does not really pay him; there are very few that breed; they have found other things pay them much better.

"Duke of Cambridge.—Why should farmers find it less profitable now than they did before?—Because the other produce pays them much better; both beef and mutton pay them much better now than they did before, and the farmers are getting into larger farms, and consequently are more engrossed in other business. Men who kept several horses before rarely keep more than just one or two now.

"Chairman.—Then, do you think that the number of farmers who breed horses has actually diminished?—Yes.

"In spite of the great increase of the demand?—Yes; a farmer cannot breed now; he has not got the materials to breed from; the foreigners have been for years buying all our best mares, consequently what he does breed he breeds from a bad mare instead of a good one; he has sold the best mare, and that has gone to Germany or Russia. They have been gradually taken away for years, and now they have drained the country so much that the farmer cannot breed, because he has not got the mare to breed from."

These are Mr. East's words, to which he adds his opinion that breeding on a large scale *cannot* be carried on profitably. We have no mares now to speak of, because "the foreigners considered our breed the best in the world," and did not care what price they paid for it. They have agents who "know England as well as we do, and they are always looking about and finding out where all the best mares are." Mr. Phillips is surprised to hear that "except during the last French war there have never been above 5,000 horses sent away from this country." It is not the foreign Governments who compete with us, but the foreign dealers. They are not limited as to price,

---

* It would not if General Peel's views were adopted.

and they buy for all purposes, military and trade. Naturally, too, they prefer mares, because these can be sold afterwards for stud purposes. When asked as to his knowledge of the export of horses to Russia, Mr. Phillips's answer is worthy of note :—

"The export of horses to Russia has been nothing in my time; but in years to come we shall have all to go to Russia for horses, for I believe it is the only country in Europe that has good horses. I know that some of our dealers have gone over now to Russia to try to buy horses, and the French dealers are going there too."

That our farmers cannot now be got to breed horses to the extent they used is Mr. Edward Greene's opinion, and on these grounds :—

"I think that the price of bullocks and sheep has acted very much upon the farmer in preventing his breeding horses; at five or three years old he makes £18 or £20 of a bullock, and he is not asked any questions as to whether it has action, or has a spavin, or whether it is a whistler, and he sells it right out; and that has led him to breed bullocks and sheep instead of horses.

"What class of men did breed principally in Norfolk and Suffolk?—The farmers breed; a man farming a large farm would have two or three mares. Then there is another great difficulty about breeding riding horses, which, perhaps, I had better turn my attention to first. Supposing a farmer begins breeding with three mares, if he is successful, before he can turn them into money at anything like a marketable price, he will have from ten to twelve animals. There will be the mares with the foals by their sides and those of the three previous years, one, two, and three year old animals, and they take a great deal of room, unless he has a quantity of poor land; and I think that now, with the advance in the price of labour, there is a good deal of poor land that would pay better for colts than it would even for bullocks, because a colt after he is a year old, if well fed the first year, which I think is a *sine quâ non*, is really better not to be too highly fed; he is less likely to throw out ringbones and spavins and splints, and those kind of things. Therefore, I think that, now that the price of horses is so much better, that kind of land will be used more for breeding purposes than it has been of late. Then he gets ten or twelve animals on to his farm, and they are a nuisance to him; unless he has a large tract of pasture he does not know what to do with his colts. They gnaw his grass and his trees, and are very troublesome to him, particularly in winter. He must have a yard specially for them; and, unless they fetch a good price, he will not put up with the inconvenience and the discomfort of having a number of young animals running about his farm."

It is not one class of horse, says the same witness, more than another which is affected by this scarcity, unless, perhaps, it may be harness horses—that is to say, "a carriage horse, a phaeton horse, or a horse to drive in a dog-cart." With hunters again it is not so noticeable, for—

"The qualifications for a hunter are not of the same description. With a hunter men put up with a good deal. A horse that will jump is called a hunter, and people manage to find horses in that way; but for a harness horse you want a certain amount of power and shape to fill the eye, and they are very difficult to get."

Mr. Church, Manager and Secretary of the General Omnibus

Company, has the same tale to tell. "Is it your impression," he is asked by the Chairman (Lord Rosebery)—

"That there is any great difficulty at the present time in procuring horses of the class that you want?—There is no doubt about it.
"Are the horses which you are working at the present moment English or foreign?—They are nearly all foreign horses at present.
"When did you first begin to procure foreign horses?—Shortly after the late war on the Continent, within about the last two years."

These foreign horses are not equal, thinks Mr. Church, to our own breed for fast work. The average amount of work to be got out of the Company's horses is from four years and a half to five years, so that Mr. Church has not yet had sufficient experience to speak of the lasting qualities of these foreigners. They are mostly Percherons, and come from Normandy and Brittany. But even this source is likely to be closed soon, owing to the increase of price the French Government have put on their stock, and then Mr. Church confesses he does not know what he shall do.

"Do they consider it perfectly hopeless to get the class of horse that you want in England?—They cannot get them; they travel for them, but they cannot get them.
"You also say that the number of working horses, in your belief, at the present time in London is greatly below that of any previous time during the last twenty years?—I believe so. I cannot give any figures to prove it, but I know that many cab proprietors and other people, who formerly kept horses, have given it up entirely, because they cannot afford to get them; in fact, they cannot get them.
"Do you mean a great many of the large cab proprietors?—No, not the large cab proprietors, but men who used to keep two or three cabs, perhaps.
"Your answer does not imply that it is because of the great demand, but because of the great scarcity of horses; it is not a relative scarcity, but an absolute scarcity?—Yes it is an absolute scarcity.
"Do you think that the scarcity is likely to increase?—I am afraid so.
"Do you think that the class of horses that you require is extensively bred in England at the present time?—I do not think it is. I am told that farmers say that it does not pay to breed horses. They prefer to breed and fatten stock, and they are not breeding horses to any extent.
"They also sell their stock to foreigners, do they not?—Yes, the foreign dealers were at the country markets, and they travelled to all the fairs, and did a vast business. There is one man named Douay, a Frenchman, who, I should think, has taken over some hundreds, and probably thousands, of horses.
"It is becoming a very serious question for your Company, is it not?—Yes, it is a question at the present time of something like £30,000.
"And, of course, if that increases very largely you will have to raise your fares very greatly, will you not, or give up your business? I am afraid that raising the fares would destroy the trade on the one hand, and, on the other, it is a very difficult question with us to know what we shall do.
"But it is a vital question, is it not?—It is, no doubt. At present we have the advantage of having very cheap provender, and have had this advantage for the last two years, and I think there is a prospect of our having it for another year. But if provender becomes dear, I could hardly tell what would be the effect upon our company."

As a set off, however, to this theory of the farmers, Colonel Maude tells us that he considers in "Cumberland, Westmoreland, and Lancashire there are more horses bred now than were bred twenty years ago." He admits there is a difficulty in buying the big horses, the Cleveland bays, used in the Royal carriages, but he attributes this to the fact that, smaller and lighter carriages being used now than was the case formerly, a lighter class of horse is required. But he says—

"I think there are more horses in the country than there ever were before. I think that there is a tremendous demand for horses—an increasing demand. There is an immense goods traffic on all the railways, and light carts and wagons, and so on, are used greatly in excess of what there ever was before. The farmers in some districts are not breeding to the extent that they used to do, but I do not know what you can do beyond giving a little reward in the shape of prizes to the farmers who breed; that would be a little stimulant, perhaps, to the breeder."

In that concluding sentence is embodied the almost universal opinion of all the witnesses as to the means whereby horse breeding and rearing may once again be established on the old footing throughout the country—premiums given by all the agricultural shows, local as well as general, not only for sires, but also for their produce. Let all the sires, those that travel through and those that are permanently located in the various districts, be first examined and approved as to their soundness. One witness, Captain Owen Slack, whose experience is chiefly in Ireland, suggests that this should be done by taxation:—*

"In the first place, I think that some action might be taken on the part of the Government to encourage breeding generally, and for that reason I think that an experiment might be tried in certain breeding districts with sires, in such counties as Kildare, or Meath, or Tipperary, or Waterford, or some of them, and these horses could be located in the district, and let out to certain approved mares at the rate that is given now by the farmers for these brutes that they have, say a sovereign. I think that would do good in one way. I think, then, that I would put a tax upon all stallions that did not receive a certificate; and if they received a certificate of soundness I would exempt them, but if not I would put the tax upon them. Then, if a man had an uncertified stallion, he would soon drop off getting mares; and you would prevent a great number of those horses being bought, for the way in which they are bought is this—it is generally some stallion that is bought at a county race meeting, perhaps a selling race, or something of that kind, and he is broken down, and £25, I should say, is the average price paid for a good number of them."

---

* The author's views are entirely concurrent with Captain Slack's; knowing that officer's assertions to be an accurate recapitulation of facts, and believing his principles to be sound and practical.

Ireland would appear to offer particular difficulties to these reformers, for we learn from Lord Doneraile that the "farmers are excessively prejudiced, and it is almost impossible to make them send to a good horse if there happens to be a popular man with a bad horse in the neighbourhood."* As a matter of fact, it must be confessed that the most emphatic advocates of this system of Government-certificated sires foresee great difficulties in the way from that prejudice which has from time immemorial been the peculiar characteristic—we were almost saying the boast—of the British farmer. Still, they none the less resolutely recommend its adoption. Mr. Phillips is very distinct on the subject :—

"The only plan that I see which is feasible is for some Government authority to be at the head to supplement the prizes of the Agricultural Society for the different classes of stallions, and give such a premium as would induce the owners of the horses to compete, and let them cover the country at two guineas a-piece as the usual price, and those horses must travel the district. It is of no use to have stationary stallions; people will not send to them. I would humbly suggest, that as Agricultural Societies are in existence, they might supplement it by a Government Commission to carry out the details, and there should be drawn up something like the system which Mr. East told the Committee was done at Glasgow. It might be easily devised that people should agree to conditions to compete for thoroughbreds, coach-horses, roadsters, and cart-horses, the same as the societies are doing now; and where they give £20 for a certain breed of horses, you will give £100 if you like. You would be sure then to get some good horses competing for the prize. The horse should be bound to serve that district which he competes for that season, at a sum not exceeding two guineas, travelling 100 miles a week in going round the same, as those men do who travel their own stallions. I would not allow them to charge more than two guineas."†

Lord Spencer, too, holds the same views, speaking, as was natural, only for the Irish side, where he admits there are complaints of the scarcity of "large, sound, weight-carrying horses." There would certainly seem to be reason in the complaint, if, as his Lordship tells us, a gentleman, willing to give any price for what he wanted, travelled all over the country last spring, and could only find two or three horses he cared to take.‡ To devote the money now yearly given for Queen's Plates, amounting to

---

* A perfect truism, and a material consideration in support of Government supervision, at least in Ireland!
† Mr. Phillips' views are good, no doubt, so far as they go, but his suggestion leaves the sire question still in the hands of individuals, not insuring a uniform standard of excellence, but only offering a reward for *the best* in what may prove (as it generally does at shows) a "rubbishing lot" of competitors.
‡ Corroborates the author's views as to degeneracy and scarcity.

a little over £1,500, to the "encouragement of agricultural societies, and the locating of stallions about the country," would, his Lordship thinks, be a decided step in the right direction—and Captain Slack is with him. A number of these plates are won by horses sent specially from England, a fact which at once destroys the very object for which these prizes were instituted—to encourage the breed of horses in Ireland. Lord Spencer considers that these Queen's Plates "cannot be defended," and "do not contribute at all to the amusements of the people."

That the good to be done by agricultural shows, and an increase in the prize-money offered, is becoming gradually recognized, we learn from Mr. Thomas Parrington, Secretary to the Yorkshire Agricultural Society. This year the Society offers prizes of £50, £20, and £10 for the best thoroughbred hunting stallions, whereas last year £30 was the highest prize. That there are not as many good horses bred in Yorkshire as formerly Mr. Parrington admits, but he is confident that the quality of what there is is as good as ever, if not better:—*

"I think the quality is wonderfully good. I was out with the Holderness hounds myself not a fortnight ago, and I counted two hundred well-mounted horsemen in the field, and I did not count them all. I asked the question what was an ordinary field thirty years ago, and they told me from twenty to thirty."

The present system of warranties and of dealers' licenses is a crying evil in the eyes of all, professional and amateur alike. Every one has to pay the license now. "What do you mean by every one?" asks the Marquis of Lansdowne of Mr. Phillips:—

"If you were to buy a horse in the country and sell it again, either at a profit or at a loss, in a week, you would be liable to the horse-dealer's license.
"Have people been called upon to pay the horse-dealer's license under those circumstances within your knowledge?—Yes. There was a case of a pig-jobber who was summoned, and I believe was convicted. He went on to the Wolds to buy some pigs, and he bought a pony; he brought it home and sold it at ten shillings profit, and he was fined £12, and had to pay the horse-dealer's license."

Mr. Lumley Hodgson, of Easingwold, in the North Riding, described by one of the witnesses as "one of the highest

---

* How superficial is this. The author knows the Holderness country and also knows that there are numbers of horse-dealing farmers attending, the "meets" on promising horses, bought far and near!!!

authorities in Yorkshire," puts in as evidence to the same effect a letter from a friend, who says:—

> "I think you know how I was used last year by the revenue officers about the horse-dealers' license. They write to me week after week insisting I should pay the duty, knowing perfectly well that I was not a horse-dealer. I told them I should do nothing of the kind; but this Government system is become such a nuisance that we farmers hardly dare sell a horse to each other, expecting to be surcharged for horse-dealing. Now I don't like being hauled up before a Magistrate as if you were a thief; I think I shall give it up altogether. My neighbour could have had £30 profit for a horse last week, but only having had him for a month he declined entirely, on account of the horse-dealing license."

And with regard to the warranty system the same witness is equally outspoken:—

> "If a dealer bought a farmer's horse, and he did not get it sold for a profit, he applied to the farmer, with an excuse that it was lame, or something, and therefore he had to return him; trusting the farmer would give him £6 or £10 sooner than have his horse back, or have a lawsuit; it was not so easy to run up and look into the truth formerly as now.
> "But, surely, if a farmer sells a horse to a dealer, and the dealer does not like him, and the dealer sends back some excuse, do you mean that he would not have him examined, or would he send him back anyway?—I mean that the farmer, sooner than stand the trial and the waste of his money in law, would rather return the dealer so much money than take the horse back.
> "Could not the farmer in the first instance either decline to warrant the horse or insist upon the horse being examined before the dealer bought him?—The dealer would not buy him unless the farmer did warrant him.
> "Could not the farmer say to the dealer, 'I will not warrant that horse, but you can have him examined by the veterinary surgeon?'—The dealer would not buy him without a written warranty.
> "He would not be satisfied with the veterinary surgeon's examination?—No.
> "Why would he not?—Because, when they could get a written warranty, they would not take the veterinary surgeon's opinion.
> "Are you speaking of first-class dealers?—Yes."

And here, in one short sentence, are Mr. Hodgson's remedies for the existing state of things, this scarcity which "has been increasing generally ever since he can recollect:"—

> "The farmers to breed, graze, and sell horses like other stock, without being subject to the dealers' license; buy three-year-old mounts for the cavalry, instead of four, because it does not pay the farmers to keep them until four years old; do away with the Queen's Plates; and give prizes at agricultural shows for good stallions; or Government to purchase good sound stallions and send them in the breeding districts to serve mares at a low price."

But after reading through the 350 pages which represent the opinions of these thirty-nine witnesses, among whom were the men best qualified, perhaps, of any throughout the length and breadth of England to speak on the subject, it seems to us that the keynote to the whole question was struck by Mr. Parrington:

> "The simple fact is that the demand exceeds the supply.

"And the demand will produce the supply in time?—No doubt it will eventually.

"It stimulates the supply?—Yes."*

That there are grievances attached to the present system of breeding and rearing, buying and selling, to be removed, and improvements to be effected, is sufficiently obvious from the evidence we have touched on. But the real grievance lies in the sudden and enormous increase of our national wealth and prosperity. For one who hunted or kept his carriage twenty or thirty years ago, it would be easy to find fifty who do so to-day. It needs but a walk down Piccadilly to the Park on any Summer evening during the London season to confirm our statement. This extraordinary demand, too, has arisen on a market already weakened by the late French war,† and tempted by the long prices offered by foreigners at a time when the reaction consequent on that mania for high prices which we can all remember had set in. We do not think, however, that the public need be under any very serious apprehension. So long as there are men to buy, we strongly suspect there will not be wanting men to sell; and to the most fearful we feel we cannot do better than recommend those comfortable words of Mr. Parrington we have already quoted, that the very fact of the demand at present exceeding the supply, will of itself stimulate the supply to rise to the demand."‡

Without attempting to review, collectively or in detail, the subject matter I have reprinted from the pages of "the leading journal" on the subject of "horse supply," I proceed with my theme after my own fashion.

The supply of horses is, admittedly, much below the requirements of the public and the War Department in this

---

* Under the lax system of breeding general horses, what benefit will that bring about, in comparison to what would be effected by the general supply of Government stallions at a period of scarcity so opportune for regenerative efforts.

† The French War had no effect upon the fashionable harness horses and hunters in use.

‡ In providing that supply, let the country be warned that "like begets like!" and take care that the *best males* are interposed at a period so exceedingly opportune to the consummation of the happiest results from such a wise and practical course.

country. In a great, energetic, and wealthy community, we might expect great things, such as that from which arises the absorbers of general horse stock in these kingdoms; but, where so great a majority of our general horses is supplied by poor farmers in Ireland, we must be careful, if we are wise, to put suitable stallions in their way, for it is sure that demand will beget supply, and that a widespread scarcity will induce to higher prices, and consequently greater inducement to breed. And any legislation calculated to ease the holders of horse stock from taxes, would assuredly be a material step in the right direction, as fostering and promoting a desire throughout the farmers and breeders to deal in more extended operations for supplying the national want. There is an imperial necessity; why not facilitate operations towards its removal by imperial countenance and aid? Let the government legislate for a national stud of stallions, to be let under licence to the general holders of stallions, with their assured *clientiel* throughout the breeding districts in Ireland and elsewhere, and by way of a start, buy up all the sires in private hands, keep the useful ones and shoot the others.

Abolish all warranties from the seller, and let the good old rule of *caveat emptor* be the guide of the purchaser. The breeder has his sunken capital, the many chances peculiar to his venture against him, before he can produce a marketable animal. It is apparent that I allude here to the breeder of general stock; for the racehorse breeder comes to market with his yearlings; whereas the other cannot, in a general way, find a customer before three, and with the army contractors not now before four! We have seen in the above extracts from *The Times*, what grievances the horse breeders may be, and are, subjected to by the present system of HORSE WARRANTY—a pernicious, ineffectual, and corrupt system; unfair on the seller, and, too often, unprotective and abortive towards the buyer.

A few words to the public may be introduced here without an unpardonable digression, as being pertinent to the subject under notice, upon the usages of horse dealing.

That King Solomon dealt in horses, the Great Book tells us, thus establishing horse dealing as of respectable antecedents and very ancient date. Also, in the 27th chapter of Ezekiel, reference is made to dealing in horses and mules in the fairs of Tarsus. We have not any record as to whether the cheating, deception, and over-reaching, which, unfortunately, has from time immemorial, justly or unjustly, been associated with the trade in the public mind, prevailed in those remote days. But English History acquaints us that so great an incubus did "coping" rascality become, an Act of the Legislature was passed in the reign of RICHARD THE SECOND, instituting a statute by which the prices of horses were regulated. Of course, such a law fell into odium and disuse, as the great individual difference in horses' value became more generally known. The legislature has long, doubtless, had a thorough knowledge of the necessity for imposing some restrictive penalty upon this branch of the national traffic; but from the many difficulties in the way, and the acrimonious jealousy, that anything like legislative interference in private affairs arouses in this country, it has never *yet* arrived at anything of a protective character more cosmopolitan and enlightened than our licensing horse traders, and our present farcical law of horse warranty.

I think a quotation from the pen of a gentleman—the Addison of his school of writing—may here be introduced with some effect, as being more free from the charge of interested motive than anybody so immediately connected with horse trade as myself, could hope to apply to his personal writing. That able penman and popular favourite, NIMROD writes: "The laws relating to selling horses, on warrantry, have been, in themselves, rendered as protective to the purchaser as we believe it is possible for words to make them. But the difficulty and uncertainty in appealing to these laws lies in the difficulty and uncertainty of proof, and which may be thus accounted for. In the first place, no evidence is so vague and contradictory as that in horse causes, and even when given by perfectly disinterested persons, merely such as are called upon professionally; secondly, from their almost general ignorance of the economy of the horse, either in theory or practice, both judges and jury often labour under very great disadvantages in their endeavours to get at the truth. Moreover, what says the warranter of a horse—and it is upon warrantry alone that an action of trover can be brought? Why, he first warrants him sound, perhaps free from vice, sometimes quiet to drive in harness, and now and then a good hunter. Now, there is no such equivocal word in the English language as the word "*sound;*" it can only be properly used with reference to an original idea or object, and is, therefore, purely an analogical word. As to its significations, they are too numerous to mention here, nor is its derivation perfectly satisfactory.

"Then, a warranty of 'free from vice,' is one of a ticklish nature. It might be very difficult to prove any real act of 'vice' in a horse while in possession of the seller; and, in the next, a horse from being ill-treated or alarmed, may become vicious in a week; never having been so before. Equally objectionable is the warranty of 'quiet in harness,' or 'a good hunter.' The horse warranted as the former may be very quiet on the day he was sold, but in a week afterwards, from some mismanagement in the driver, from sudden alarm, or from some of the harness pinching him, he may become a kicker or a runaway. The hunter also may be good for one man, and not worth a shilling to another; all depending upon the pace at which he is ridden after hounds." So has written the astute and classic Nimrod in his work "THE HORSE AND HOUND;" and he continues the subject to a considerable extent, taking care to give the following caution and advice—not to trust to the glorious uncertainty of law; but to be always provided with the most experienced and honest professional man you can procure, to examine for unsoundness on your behalf before purchase, and with a practical friend or agent, as to the animal's "points," action, capacity for, and adaptability to, the purpose for which he is being purchased. Our author says:—"*In fact, as knowledge in horseflesh can only be the result of experience, we strongly recommend all inexperienced purchasers not to rely on their own judgments!*" Previous to the establishment of my Agency,* nearly twenty years ago, I am not aware that "inexperienced" horse buyers had any resource in this most helplessly pitiable of all incapacities, except they fell back upon the dubious ability of an acquaintance; or the assumed ability, and, too generally, venal assistance of their groom or coachman. And what is the common extent of a "friend's" knowledge? He can tell you a riding horse from a clothes horse! But his assumption is magnificent, and inflated in proportion to your own ignorance. It don't proceed from a desire to hurt you. But we are all *weak* on this subject. You can canvass our musical ability; sneer at our artistic taste; ignore our professions of general knowledge; pronounce our authority in Havanahs nil; and our taste in wines erroneous. We Britons can patiently endure and forgive this; but question the man's judgment in horse flesh, who fancies himself in that line, and you have to the greatest certainty made a mortal enemy! It is not only a

---

* NOTE.—See Appendix for Terms and Testimonials.

weakness but a passion in these Islands to be "horsey," or considered so. Look how many there are who really don't know which side to mount a horse from, that dress as if they were a cross between a swell and a pad-groom. Some such caricature as gave rise to the definition I have read somewhere, "*he was the horsiest man on foot; and the footiest man on a horse I have ever seen.*" Such persons, however, are comparatively harmless to the public, but, where we find people with the ignorance of the know-nothing announce themselves as competent assistants to the public in search of horses, it is quite time to raise the finger of warning, and suggest that before submitting to the potent influences of effrontery and emblazonment it would be well to investigate carefully the respective pretensions and credentials of every man holding himself forth as a "Horse Commissioner." Quack doctors and charlatans come under the ban of the law, but, unhappily for the public, there is no legal restriction to penalize the bold but ignorant assumers of a profession, calling, or trade, that great quick-ness of perception, early association, and the devotion of a life-time can alone make the proficient in. Surely, if agents offering themselves in the horse market are competent for the present, they must have been in the past, and if so, they must be able, somehow, to satisfactorily prove it. Why then not seek for such proof?

But, I must apologize; the matter is to me a personal and a sore one, and has led me from the track I was journeying in.

The subject of horse-warranty is one of vital importance in the present consideration of "horse supply," and all that can induce to its satisfactory promotion. Protect the pro-ducer—therefore the vendor—and let the customer guard himself by trial with veterinary and public agency supervi-sion. The tender mercies of vendors are, no doubt, not desirable concessions if any truth resides in the doctrine of Pomponius, or, the tenets of Erasmus; the former tells us "The law of nature allows of over-reaching in buying and selling;" while the latter would appear to give a "general absolution" in the following words:—

> "Scis quanta impostura sit, apud nos,
> In his qui vendunt equos."

The facility that is given by existing usage to any person competent, or not, to offer himself as an agent for the suffrages of the public in horse buying and selling, has assisted in no immaterial way to cast disrepute upon horse-dealing transactions to a vastly greater extent than is generally understood. This is much to be lamented, as in the present day it is not easy to name a public servant that would be more desirable and useful than a thoroughly practical, energetic, and conscientious man, with sufficient competency for selection of horses, at a time when exceptional scarcity, and consequent dearness, debars the possibility of the amateur purchaser suiting himself independent of the expensive intervention of the horse-dealer. And when we reflect upon the large responsibility, the great opportunity offered for remunerative dishonesty to such a person as a horse-agent, is it too much to expect that such a calling should be only eligible to individuals whose capacity could be proved, as in other professions, and the exercise of whose offices could only be legitimately rendered under license; such license to be restricted to men who could furnish the most satisfactory evidence of their eligibility and "straight sailing" in the line they were devoted to.

In our time any unprincipled person unable to compete with an established agent in a fair way, can covertly set malignity and slander to defame a rival he detests, because of proved superiority. And we all know how such things, like the schoolboys' snowball, gather as they go.

> "Rumour is many-tongued, I wis:
> "And they do well who thus depict her;
> "She is the sister unto babbling echo,
> "Their common parentage is empty sound,
> "Then give no heed to flying rumour!"

The old play writer above quoted, is terse and graphic, but, notwithstanding the monition in his concluding lines, this charitable world does too often "give ear" to slander of public men, without evincing the common morality to investigate the source and cause from which, what too often would prove to be interested and mendacious, charges of malversation spring. Grant a man in any walk of life the accident of having by some signal individuality taken precedence of others, and "envy, hatred, malice, and all uncharitableness," are too surely launched at him.

Licenses for horse-agents would go far to remove the consequence of such procedure; for there would be a guarantee to the public that a duly authorized person had given evidence of his eligibility, in a *prima facie* way, at least, and of his right to be regarded as a fit and trustworthy person. In absence of anything of the kind, the horse market is so over-run with objectionable characters, while at the same time hard-working, honest, and clever judges are to be found, that the only safety for the public fortunately remains in their own hands; namely, trust no man, no matter what appearances may be, without he can produce evidence unimpeachable of his status, from recorded experiences of his clients in the past, and personal references in the present.

Whatever a man's struggles and trials in private life may be are his own affairs; but, in dealing with the public, it is only fair to expect, where much confidence is a necessity of his business, that, as a public man, he should be prepared to show himself worthy of it. And he who can produce such evidence in a clear, satisfactory manner, has much to complain of in a state of the law where, with less study, and not one-tenth of the experience devoted to acquirement of competency, other professions are protected and his is not.

In the event of the contemplated change in, or abolishment of law of warranty, just look at what a boon to the aristocracy would be an agency based upon capacity and integrity alone, that for a reasonable charge would undertake all the disagreeability and critical duty of selection for approval of intending buyer, and, if approved, subsequent negotiation, trial, purchase, and delivery. Such an agency has mine been for nearly twenty years, and such do other aspirants to public favour profess theirs to be. If competency and trustworthiness were alone permitted to offer for public support under a license as in other professions, I have no doubt but that the business of a faithful, competent, and appreciated horse agent would rival in emolument a fashionable doctor's annual fees, or the income of many busily employed silk gowns. The Augœan stable required the labours of a Hercules to clean, and, verily, as in our degenerate times no such physical aid can be brought to bear, if even it would apply, the slough into which horses, &c., have at length fallen will want a mighty power of a cathartic and regenerating character to set things straight again.

High prices now maintaining for horses of soundness and character will, no doubt, lead to stimulation in breeding and increased returns throughout these kingdoms of horse stock for general and war purposes. But supply thus induced will as certainly find a commensurate balance some day, and without a revivifying principle we may, in a few *years*, find ourselves upon the horns of a similar dilemma.

The most material thing to be considered in contemplating the solidity of anything is its base. Upon that the whole structure rests, and, in cases of physiological construction, entirely depends. We have seen that money will procure us the right STALLIONS, and it is a conceded fact that the stallion's power upon posterity is, possibly, cent. per cent. more important than the mare's. Notwithstanding which, it would be a fallacious attempt to breed from objectionable mares. I am in a position to assert, and with all courtesy but firmness to challenge contradiction, that, so long as THE FOREIGNER is the better buyer for our young mares—as previous incontestible evidence pronounces him to be—than the breeder can find amongst his own countrymen in our open fairs and marts, so long are we, especially in Ireland, *sure to have only the refuse of the market to fulfil the important duties of stud matrons.* Now then, as this statement admits of no contradiction in fact, in what position do we find ourselves? I need scarcely answer. It is patent to the reader. We must restrict the facilities permitted foreigners (those excellent judges) from taking our choicest mares, and the country *must* supply a class of sires to the general horse breeder at a tempting tariff that it is impossible for private enterprize to effect. Investors in stallions are parsimonious, except in the few instances where gentlemen of wealth keep a horse for the use of their tenants—and, even then, alas!—too often the first thing considered is what will be the price. The speculator in sires for public use at the very moderate prices that farmers will consent to pay, go in for pedigree and winning brackets in the index to "Weatherby," "rather than for those intrinsic and imperative qualifications of colour, bone, size, action, and quality," that are the considerations alone admissible in the selection of a horse for the pro-creation of sound and valuable stock. Where these qualities are procurable in a thorough-bred stallion he is quite worth 500 guineas, and, if got for much less, the man that sells him is far an easier "parter" than I should be if his owner.

If the legislature interposes there are only two concurrent and practicable sources open for beneficial utilization in the breeding and improvement of war and general horses, good mares, and suitable stallions, and, if it don't, *Fascilis descensus Averni !*

The next consideration is for the holders of our general brood mares. Penalise the consumer as much as you like, but foster, protect, and cherish the producer by all the encouraging and sustaining legislation you can cast around him. Let the buyer take care of himself—as it is just and reasonable he should—but let the country take care of the breeders and farmers; the horse-dealers and "customers" are quite match enough for each other, and long odds as outsiders may think it upon the successors of Solomon and the House of Togarmah, I may truthfully say the respectable men of the London trade are far "more sinned against than sinning." Lords, bishops, lawyers, parsons, doctors, sailors, and soldiers have all to be satisfied and kept in good temper too often contrary to justice, reason, and common sense, because men will only see with their own eyes *sometimes*. Licenses, heavy rents, immense provender and wages accounts have to be paid; servants (the harpies) have to be *tipped;* veterinary surgeons have to be feed; "dead uns" and "roarers" have to be put on to the live and sound ones; breeders demand prices never heard of before, and, in this expensive and exceptional state of things, West End dealers, who must provide the *creme de la creme* of the *equine* race for their stables, are too often pronounced by selfish and unthinking gentlemen extortionate in their demands. It is now a good time, we come upon, for consideration of all these things, for where can we expect redress in such matters if not from our present House of Commons, so aptly termed "The 'Squires Parliament"? If, happily, legislative efforts be made, let us hope that they will be general and not partial. It will not be quite enough to produce in improved character and greater quantities the sort of horses we now lack, if we do not endeavour to render trade relations concerning them purer, more popular and feasible. To do so we have only to pay the same amount of respect and attention to the principles which direct and the laws that govern horse-trading that we do to some other commercial pursuits.

Before any one can be capable of guarding others against errors and impositions, he must first make himself master perfectly of in what the evils consist, and how fraud and injustice is practised. To shield others, experience in the cases from which danger may result will suffice; but to detect the means by which objectionable practices are put into operation, it becomes imperative to have been brought much into contact with circumstances that give rise to their operation, and to have from actual experience derived an intimate knowledge of the system and machinery that operate to foster and support the dishonest man at the expense of his upright and comparatively helpless neighbour. Then, and not till then, is any person or *body* qualified to give beneficial hints, or make salutary laws conducive to the protection of the unwary or inexperienced, and to the general credit of the horse-trade when in the hands of dangerous persons.

I now approach a portion of my subject that I cannot, like the druggist's pills, wrap in silver leaf, for the purpose of permitting the cathartic and invigorating principle of the compound to come into active and salutary operation without imparting (to a certain class) a taste of the bitter. But as classes, as well as individuals, are but units to be sacrificed to the great total of public weal; though, as a man, I may deplore the necessity that inflicts pain upon others, no matter how unworthy; yet, as a public servant, sympathy for anything, or persons, not according to straightforward principles is incompatible with that position, and therefore beyond the pale of solicitude.

Upon the face of the habitable globe there cannot be found to exist among any class of men greater infamy, lower villany, deeper cunning, more skilful hypocrisy, and more daring dishonesty than amongst a large majority of those who get their livelihood in connection with horses. It is supererogatory to remark that in the horse trade are to be found many, the propriety and respectability of whose transactions will bear comparison with any trade or profession in existence; *par exemple*, such men as George Rice, Ned Fowler, John Renison, and Little Sheward, &c., &c.

From out the phalanx of unscrupulous talent, however, are drawn *habitués* of the LIVERY and COMMISSION YARDS; and, notwithstanding that many proprietors of such places do all that a strong desire to act fairly by their constituents can prompt, to exclude objectionable characters from their premises, their utmost efforts are abortive of their object, as it is a delicate as well as a dangerous course of operation to attempt to fix a stigma upon any individual, except direct proof of culpability is at the disposal of the accuser. And, for very obvious reasons in such cases it cannot be relied upon, no matter how strong individual opinion and individual evidence may be.

The owners of such establishments *may be* unimpeachable; they may strive with might and main and purest purpose to purge their public yards of the moral rottenness and practical villany that pervade them. But "right is not might." The accumulations of stable abominations in ancient times required the fabled aid of a mythical deity to cleanse, and as in our day moral strength and power rather than physical force must be applied to effectuate a parallel though dissimilar purification, it is by the force alone of reason, enlightenment, and public opinion such a desirable object as the abolition of present irregularities (a mild phrase for the sleepless scheming that pervades and surcharges livery, commission, and auction marts where such characters as I hint at "most do congregate") can be attained.

Private sellers and buyers suffer a common grievance from the reason of wrong to both. A majority of vendors and purchasers of horses have heretofore felt their inferiority of judgment in such dealings, while only the common means of redress (if redress it can be called) was at their option. How were they guarded? What resources had they? The buyer was all right so long as he could afford to pay the prices which a first-class dealer's enormous expenses necessarily demands. Truly, the expensive but respectable horse-dealer is a boon to the wealthy, and but for the many extraneous circumstances that compel him to charge "two prices," might also be useful to less favoured sons of fortune. But he must charge extravagantly, or submit to be ruined. His legitimate expenses are something colossal, his risks appalling; and, let us add, his outgoings for "Tip" beyond computation. To secure custom and sales he has not only to please his intending purchaser, but the *friends* (?) who are often seen at the elbows of the great: the groom, the coachman, and the helpers too, are hypophagists. To meet the rapacity of "hangers-on," retainers, &c., the dealer is in self-defence compelled to "put it on," by asking and getting more than his horse is worth intrinsically, else he should have to pay the indispensable "tip" from legitimate profits, which would be simply ruinous! Who suffers by all this? Why, the buyer, who, either begrudging the moderate legitimate fee of a clever "commissioner," whose practical experience renders his valuation accurate, or dreading that "tip" would find its way to an agent's pocket that would be so madly unmindful of his own interests and the welfare of his business as by any such dereliction from a straight course to put himself and his reputation in the power of the seller, goes alone, and pays the penalty of this "too clever by half" kind of policy through his banker's account.

So much for wealthy purchasers, and leaving less rich ones to contend with the various chances of being swindled by "copers," "chaunters," improvised "trustees to a gentleman deceased," *et hoc genus omne*, we shall just glance at the position which private sellers occupy. They have few alternatives. In some instances the owners are conversant with horses, and really know a hunter and hack from a buggy horse. But their position and opportunity too frequently preclude them from attaining to that nice discernment in *equine* trading which leads a practical judge to value a horse with the same trade accuracy that a grocer should a hogshead of sugar, or a butcher a fat bullock. The consequence being that very frequently they have the mortification to discover, when too late, that either a sale had been effected much under value, or that a liberal offer had been unwisely refused. There are many gentlemen whose position in society and habits in life, whose health and tastes render them totally unfit for the arduous, irritating, and disagreeable duties of salesmen of horses. In such cases one of two expedients is only open, if they do not wisely employ a competent and trustworthy HORSE COMMISSIONER, namely, entrust their property to the management of servants, who, as a rule, are self-sufficient and incompetent in such transactions, *if not worse*, or to consign their horses for sale to some public mart.

We have, all of us who visit such places, seen hanging about horse auction marts, from year's end to year's end, a lounging but vigilant-looking lot of fellows, whose peculiar "get up" is sufficiently characteristic to assign them their unenviable *grade*, without any display of their tastes and habits through their conversation. If the knocker-knees and tight-fitting trousers be not present to proclaim their identity, and the gaudy scarf or ash-plant be laid aside, the peculiar and jauntily-carried hat, or some other salient and inseparable *et cetera* of the low horse dealer's external man will surely be there to proclaim to the *cognoscenti*, as with the voice of a stentor, the presence of one or more of those industrious and unscrupulous individuals that has been well but inelegantly described as "a cove with his weather-eye open, *invariably* looking out for squalls;" while to the uninitiated and simple, they pass merely for what they seem—men about horses. Amongst persons of this appearance, however, will be found the hard-working, industrious, "as-honest-as-I-can" kind of poor fellow; but he is "as snow in summer," as "angels' visits," a white black-bird, or anything else *very rare*. These fellows are mostly an organized gang, whose object is to prevent sales of valuable and useful horses from being effected, until by their efforts the horse's character is so injured that he must either fall a prey much under value to some of the clique, or be removed unsold after the heavy expenses of livery, advertisement, travelling, &c., has been paid by the unfortunate owner. This is technically called "crabbing." They do nothing openly that can be effected secretly, and thus their delinquencies, though well known to exist, are permitted to remain unmolested. Besides, looking at the thing in a business point of view, they buy and sell many horses, are ready cash customers; and it is therefore wiser in the estimation of even some proprietors from whom the public have a right to expect a higher code of morality, not to look out at the "corners of their eyes" for objects that will not offend their vision if they gaze before them in the ordinary way of such persons. Under such a dispensation, how can we be surprised at the constant and long accruing complaints of breeders of general horses as to what an unprofitable speculation that is, where, after the production of the commodity, there are so many obstacles to its remunerative disposal through such a common channel for forcing a market. So, with organized villany to impede the seller, and incapacity in judgment that leaves the buyer too open to the ruse of the "chaunter," and numerous other objectionable and potent *impedimenta*, it needs not one to be much skilled in the mysteries of Demoivre and the doctrine of chances to discern that "the odds" are all against the gentlemen and breeders, and that an honest and efficient agent for their mutual protection, under the existing state of things, is a practical necessity of the times, and that such a man cannot fail to enlist influential support, and, if true to his mission, soar above the united animosity of slander and malevolence from the interested or the envious detraction that is a natural consequence of his position.

The difference, too, between the agent who has no interest at conflict with his client and the commissioner who keeps livery stables, is well worth consideration. The only possible benefit that can arise to the former will proceed only from a sale, so that the sooner he brings a buyer to the stable of the owner the sooner will he derive the benefit arising from the only possible source of emolument to *him*, namely, the sale of the animal. Thus giving at once between such agent and his employer a community of interest. The large profits arising from livery bills are matters of irritating notoriety to consigners.

CHAPTER VIII.

It is apparent to the trained reader, that the production of these pages evince anything but an attempt at concise book-making; as the thoughts arise they have been jotted down without any regularity or order, not at all in the hope of making a well ordered little volume, but with the intention of getting rid of something the writer very badly wanted to say. This may be accepted as an explanation why I have introduced matter not directly applying to the main feature of the book, though somewhat pertinent thereto.

A vexed question that has had much valuable ventilation in that excellent country gentleman's journal, *The Field*, recently, is that of horse-warranty and horse examinations. I have before said a word or two on the subject of SOUNDNESS, and I do not like to omit my views as to examinations by Veterinary Surgeons. What is it a buyer wants? A sound horse! What is a sound horse? He must be physically capable of discharging the duties, well and continuously for a reasonable time, for which he has been selected with a view to purchase. Ought not that to be all that a buyer should require? But, is it so? Certainly it is not! There are some Veterinary Surgeons with sufficient common sense and good feeling to recommend horses that in their professional capacity they cannot give a "clean certificate" with. But there are others notorious for not only rejecting horses for the most trivial and unimportant things, having nothing at all to do with soundness, but filling up their certificates with observations not at all belonging to the province of a qualified and respectable M.R.C.V.S. What do we expect of a Veterinary Surgeon when we ask his advice as to soundness? What is his duty in such case? Simply, that he inspects the horse for *disease* and lameness; and, if free from these, he is *professionally sound*. Once the veterinary descends to observations outside, or rather beneath his professional status, he volunteers an office that neither duty or propriety demands of him. If a gentleman, or tradesman, has had the trouble of showing his horse, and submitting him to a trial more or less arduous, and that he has sold him "subject to a Vet.'s opinion," he ought to expect he is bringing his horse to such establishments to be professionally examined for disease, and not for the purpose of undergoing a second overhauling for the very qualifications he has already satisfied the intending buyer about. But in notorious instances the nuisance of this derogation from professional conduct has become quite a standing grievance. This is a great pity, for, no doubt, the error is committed from over zeal and not a desire for the publicity of a hypercritical character that induces to large practice with intending purchasers.

It is quite time that something like a rule, or a law, should be come to upon the subject of soundness or unsoundness in horses; for while left an open question as to what constitutes it, it is plain that opinion in many cases will be varied according to the order of mind rather than the professional capacity of the inspectors; and an individual experience so varied, old, and practical as mine has been, enables me to declare that if any given horse be subjected to the professional inspection of four leading veterinary surgeons, the odds are that they will not be unanimous in opinion.

As our Courts of Law have been too frequently made the arena for questions as to soundness, it will be expedient to look at the views taken by some of our ablest legal authorities upon the subject.

Chief Justice Best, in the case of Best *v.* Osborne, held that "sound" meant perfect.

Mr. Baron Parke said—"The word 'sound' means what it expresses, namely, that the animal is sound and free from disease at the time he is warranted;" and in the same case, Mr. Baron Alderson said—"The word 'sound' means *sound*, and the only qualification of which it is susceptible arises from the purpose for which the warranty is given."

A horse may be defined to be "sound" when he is free from hereditary disease, is in possession of his natural physical powers and constitutional health, and has as much bodily perfection as is consistent with his individual formation; which latter consideration is the province of the purchaser, and not of the veterinary examiner, except specially retained to combine with his professional duties an extraneous office.

Lord Ellenborough said—"It has been held by very high authority (Sir James Mansfield, C I.) that roaring is not necessarily unsoundness, and I (Lord Ellenborough) entirely concur in that opinion. If the horse emits a loud noise which is offensive to the ear, merely from a bad habit which he has contracted, or from any cause which does not interfere with his general health or muscular powers, he is still to be considered a sound horse. On the other hand, if the *roaring* proceeds from any disease, or organic infirmity, which renders him incapable of performing the usual functions of a horse, then it does constitute unsoundness. The plaintiff has not done enough in showing that this horse was a roarer. To prove a breach of warranty, he must go on to show that the roaring was symptomatic of disease."

Mr. Baron Parke says—"If the disease was not of a nature to impede the natural usefulness of the animal for the purpose for which he is used—as, for instance, if a horse had a slight pimple on his skin, it would not amount to *unsoundness;* but even if such a thing as a pimple were on some parts of the body where it might have that effect —for instance, on a part which would prevent the putting a *saddle* or *bridle* on the animal, it would then be different."

Now, with all this "rubbish" confronting us from the judicial bench, is it not apparent that simple and effective legislation, comprehensive in theory and handy in practice, is demanded? A careful perusal of all the trials upon veterinary jurisprudence for a quarter of a century that have come under my notice, have led me to form the opinion that an effective measure may be arrived at for the abolition of conflicting evidence and judicial ignorance in "horse cases."

I would abolish warranty altogether, as the very root of all the trouble, perjury, worry, and infamy, that characterise litigations arising from sale and purchase of horses. I would substitute for it a liberal trial, dependent for its duration upon *the fitness* of the individual animal. For what might be only a "bit of exercise" for a horse "in work," would, too often, result in the ruin of a valuable animal prepared and standing for sale. After the trial, the soundness or unsoundess of the horse remained with the veterinary surgeon selected by the purchaser to examine for him.

A veterinary surgeon is placed in the position of, say, a solicitor. The party requiring his services is his *client* for the time during which the professional is exercising his offices upon his behalf. Of course, if the buyer instructs his adviser to examine for *legal* soundness, he knows his duty. But, where so many really valuable horses for the purpose for which their qualifications and education adapt them are not *legally* sound, how much more expedient is it for an intending buyer to say to the "Vet.," "I have agreed to purchase this horse for such or such work, have the goodness to look him over, and say is there anything to prevent this animal proving serviceable?" Look what a lot of useless verbiage and consequent bewilderment in the minds of a majority of buyers this would get rid of! They do not want to know that a horse has "a speck on his eye," a "slight splent," a "small foot," or "an incipient spavin;" "has a hoarseness in his breathing," or "makes a whistling noise, and is, consequently, unsound." He may have one, or all those infirmities, and be still worth a lot of money. Get rid of technicalities and *legal* soundness, and let these questions be dependent upon the opinion of the professional selected by the purchaser to do duty for him. Let the general understanding be that, if such men as Messrs. Mavor, Field, South, Cox, Mr. Stevens, Mr. Williams, and such other respectable London practitioners can say, "I have examined this horse and I think he will, or I think he won't, serviceably discharge the duties for which you propose to buy him," then, I say, let *that* be final and conclusive one way or other!

Such a course would reduce the now complicated system of buying and selling horses to a very open, fair, and general matter of barter and sale. Would free the breeders from an incubus too heavy for them to bear, as having been notoriously perverted against them by horse-dealers; and do more to give a stimulus, so desirable, to the breeding and keeping of horse-stock by farmers and country gentlemen for sale than we can at all imagine. Supplement this by total abolishment of horse-dealers' licence, and the penalizing with the necessity of license HORSE COMMISSION AGENTS, and a very short time, I think, would show the value of any such course of action towards stimulating the horse supply in these kingdoms.

To avoid misconception, I may observe, I am aware that Horse Commission Agents that keep livery stables have been held to be liable to pay Horse-Dealers' duty, but those who act as Agents, and have no stables, go "scot free," a very premium upon adventure.

CHAPTER IX.

ANCIENT and modern writers, from the dawn of civilization to the imperial crowning of "William the Divine," at Versailles, have had included amongst those writing on horses and horse matters, statesmen, philosophers, rural-economists, poets, historians, sportsmen, veterinarians, physiologists, and variously impregnated amateurs. From the time of Job, through Homer, Xenophon, Aristotle, and Herodotus, on through the works of Buffon, Cuvier, and Bell, and hosts of others, the horse has, from one motive or another, been the object of careful investigation, and frequently vivid and poetic as well as practical and exhaustive description. It is questionable, however, that the enquiry, though long and minute, has had more of research of a general character regarding the natural history of the animal than with regard to his strictly domestic relations to man, in his subjugated and *improved* state, dealing with those characteristics and attributes that an advanced civilization and the modern requirements of war, fashion, or sport, together with the demands of commercial and agricultural pursuits call for, as all important to us as a people in these work-a-day and shifting times of the nineteenth century.

Like the Irish postillion who keeps a gallop for the avenue, with the wise and laudable view of pleasing his "fare" before the important moment, to the Jehu, of parting for the day, so I have reserved for my closing page the Briareus-handed power wielded by Mr. Edmund Tattersall in anything regarding questions of "horse supply." It is not only that in *him* is now concentrated all the fame of the world-wide institution of which he remains "the bright particular star," but that personally he has secured for himself, by individual worth through a life of signal ability, coupled with strictest integrity, the approved respect and friendship of both great and small. For amongst the "small talk" that one is sure to hear in all classes connected with horses about "Tattersall's," and all connected with it, whatever may be the observations with regard to others, there is but one verdict when his name is mentioned—"Oh, Tattersall is a gentleman, and a thundering good fellow into the bargain." I, therefore, thought, and think, that at the "wind up" of my chat with the reader, nothing could prove more agreeable and interesting than a *résumé* from "Mr. Edmund's" out-spoken opinions upon a congenial occasion on the subject we are engaged with.

MR. E. TATTERSALL ON THE SUPPLY OF ENGLISH CAVALRY HORSES.

Read before the Farmers' Club, Monday, March 6th, 1871.

IN introducing to the Farmers' Club this important subject, Mr. Tattersall read a letter, written by him in the summer of 1870, and published in *Bell's Life* on September the 10th, of the same year. "I shall have," said Mr. Tattersall, in his speech to the Farmers' Club, "the opportunity of reading to you letters, and giving you information from the highest authorities in Prussia and in Austria, showing you what the enlightened governments of those countries have done, and are doing; and thus, I think, you will come to the conclusion that, as in other things, we Englishmen are not placed in our right position, and therefore lose *caste* in Europe. As we have upwards of 30 millions of the bravest people in the world, and no efficient army—as we have the finest volunteer force in the world, and it is snubbed and kept down by military jealousy—as we have the best engineers and mechanics, and are short of guns and short of powder, as in all other things with us unready Saxons, so it is with our Cavalry. We have the best breed of horses in the world, sought after by all other countries, and yet our Cavalry are badly mounted, and are not what they ought to be! and for all this who is to blame? Why the people at large—you amongst the rest—who ought to speak out through your members of Parliament, and through the "press;" and let those know who manage your affairs, that above all things we *will have* an effective army, ample guns, artillery of the best, with horses of the best class to draw them, without which they are useless; and cavalry horses of the highest class, to mount our cavalry soldiers upon, with ample reserves, which in cavalry is most important; for though we may buy horses in haste for draught horses, you cannot make a horse a broke charger under a year or two, any more than you can a good cavalry soldier to ride him. Let us then have no more cheese-paring Chancellors of the Exchequer; they do not pay in the long run any more than other cheap articles. Let us have the best horses at any cost; it is the cheapest in the end, and all the money is spent amongst the farmers and breeders who pay the Queen's taxes. At the present moment, under sudden pressure, we require a much larger number of cavalry chargers than usual. As the late Lord Hobart said, we are always vibrating between parsimony and panic. Just now we are something in the latter stage—in other words we are not prepared; we want 4,000 horses; 2,000 of them for artillery, for which £40 each will be given. These they may get, but *there will be much difficulty in getting the other 2,000 for cavalry, such as they ought to be, to carry heavy weights long distances,** and without that they are useless for work of war, and not fit for much in time of peace, and when you have got them they will take from one to two years to make.

---

* NOTE.—Does not this assertion, from such a source, impress the reader with the justice of the author's theory as to degeneracy in our breed of general horses.

About 30,000 horses have gone from England to France during the war. At the time our Government ("the blessed Liberals") were hesitating about giving £40 each for 2,000 artillery horses, Gambetta sent an order to give from £45 to £50 for 2,000. And this, I suppose, decided our authorities to give £40; so that we may thank Gambetta for getting us a better article.

In the Crimean war £40 was given; since then the price came down to £30 for three-year-olds, and £35 for four-year-olds; then no four-year-olds were bought at the time except they could be bought at the same price. Farmers and breeders would sell useful lean three-year-olds early in the year for £30, but would not keep them till four at anything like the same price, as they found useful horses worth £40 or more. Then the Prussians and Austrians came into the market, and bought up all the quick, active horses, at from £35 to £40, or £45 each. *In seven years, from the two ports of Hull and Harwich alone, about* 14,000 *mares were sent off!* These were the mares which we ought to have retained to breed from. They are the very things we now want. If one-half only had remained to become brood mares, we ought to have had, at least, 5,000 *horses per annum from them*, and they would most of them have remained in the country *had the price given for our troop horses been £5 higher;* therefore you are suffering from the effect of buying a low-priced and inferior article in two ways. Most of the light troopers, of late years, *have been purchased* in Ireland, at about £30. The price given has not been enough to induce breeders to breed and keep good animals for the purpose of the army, more especially as the demand has been small and intermitting,* instead of remunerative and continuous.

The mares are gone, and *it will take years to replace them.*† The price of horses, like everything else, is higher in England than elsewhere, and is not likely to be cheaper, but dearer. Upwards of 60,000 were eaten in Paris. How many were used up

---

* Why should it be so with a large per centage of our cavalry soldiers on foot, and our Artillery inefficiently horsed? The author don't know. Better ask the "blessed Liberals!"

† Thank our stars for that, if we only replace them, as we may do, with improved quality.

and eaten during the war it is impossible to say, but it must leave a very large demand in the future.

As our farmers and breeders can grow cattle and sheep of any size or shape, and to the greatest perfection, *so can they grow horses of any stamp ;** but they must be grown to pay, or they will not be grown by men who have got their living to get by their business.

The sort of animals we want to carry troopers is a short-legged, active hunter, not the Leicestershire horse, but the horse for the shires and chase counties. This horse, good of his kind, is worth 50 to 60 guineas in a fair at four years old, and many of them 100 guineas or more. (The author has seen them sell for 200 and 250 guineas.) How, then, can they be got for £80 at three years old, and for £40 at four years old, except the inferior animals that dealers and others won't buy? Such a horse as I have described ought to be able to carry 16 stone from London to Brighton (fifty miles) in the day, and back to London the next . . . . but where would you find a trooper's horse to do it? or how many out of one hundred of them would get to Brighton and back in two days? If they cannot do this they are not efficient, and therefore valueless in an emergency.

As far as I can ascertain, we have not more than 10,000 cavalry, and those only on paper. What the real number of horses trained to their work, and fit to carry men, I have no means of knowing; but as we want 4,000 this year, or much more than one-third of the whole amount, it looks as if the parsimonious fit had been 'a long one this time, and therefore now requires a large and sudden outlay. In Prussia and Austria the calculation is about 10 per cent. annually, so that we ought really to want 1,000. As we want 4,000, it is 40 per cent. in lieu of 10, and this is what they call economy!

In Austria and Prussia they have all they want—and reserves. They are ready; we are not. Which is the best and cheapest in the end?

I will tell you, gentlemen, what they do in Austria, and I get my information from an officer of cavalry, who was a great

---

* NOTE.—Bravo! Mr. Tattersall, that is the point. But they won't do so without they can get the proper seed for the desired crop.

many years in the Austrian Service, and one of the best judges of horses met with, and who was constantly employed for purchase of horses for the cavalry in Austria, and of horses, stallions, and mares (thorough-bred), obtained from this country for the Austrian Government, and who has attended many of our agricultural shows. The Colonel tells me that they have about 4,000 stallions covering *gratis*, or at a mere nominal fee, for the Government. They have no prior claim on the produce. The re-mount department of the State purchases, as any one else, in the open market, at about the following prices:—Heavy cavalry and heavy artillery at about £32; light cavalry, £25; pack horses, £15. I believe they buy nothing under four or five years old. In 1854, he purchased in one district for the re-mount 15,000 horses in about four weeks at those prices, and good useful horses, which were all passed by the officers appointed, who are very particular.

There are several public breeeding studs.

The stud at Kisberr was established by the present Emperor, and is entirely of English blood. For this stud were bought Buccaneer for 3,000 guineas; Ostregor, I sold for 8,000 guineas; Teddington (Derby winner), 1,400 guineas; Daniel O'Rourke (Derby winner), 800 guineas; Sabreur, Codrington, Oakball, and others, high-class thorough-bred horses, amounting from twenty to twenty-five in number, all bought since 1860. Forty thorough-bred mares were purchased for this stud at an average of 200 guineas each, at Sir Tatton Sykes's sale alone, and many others partly thorough-bred, partly half-bred mares, amounting to between 300 and 400. Besides, the Colonel purchased in two or three years about 150 mares, the best of the old Irish blood, for Austria. *He would not buy half-bred English mares, however good-looking, for this stud, because he could not depend on their back blood, and was afraid of their throwing back to the cart or under-bred horse*, and so prove soft and slow and therefore bad.

From this stud, commencing from the best stallions from England, are bred the stallions which are sent into the country to breed from, so that Austria and Hungary deserve to have, and have good horses.

Recent events have taught us, with the stern logic of facts as startling as the world ever saw, that, believing in the doctrine of universal peace, we have been living in a fool's paradise. The Millennium has not yet come—the lion has not lain down with the lamb—and when he does, as the Yankee said, "I guess the lamb will be *inside the lion!*"

We must be like the strong man armed, especially in cavalry and artillery, and then, once more, we shall be feared and respected by our neighbours, and the "Civis Romanus Sum" of Lord Palmerston will be no idle boast when once more it is understood, that the same meaning is conveyed in the words—"I am an Englishman."

In the handling of our present subjects, I have deemed it desirable and interesting to trace from remote sources the "changes and chances" that have given to us that noble type of the *equus caballus* that has long distinguished the British Isles, remarking upon the causes that produced him, and pointing to the existing and accruing dangers that have degenerated and threaten to effectually deteriorate him if pursued. My main object, however, has been to keep my theme before the reader, so that when dealing with pertinent matter thereto, it might be considered that my research or digression was more with the view "to point a moral than to adorn a tale."

I hope to have not, at least, failed to impress the reader with the undoubted axiom and matter of most important consideration, that it is preferable and wiser to have that source from which good or evil must necessarily proceed of such character and merit as will insure beneficial rather than deleterious results; and that to provide us with sound, stout, and reliable horses for our exigencies in peace or war, it is incontestably necessary to take care that the parents, especially the males, are of as fine, pure, and sound a type as can be procured. Reader, I submit I have established this; and before closing the subject of our nervous consideration, I must once more ask you to consider, *per contra*, what have we to look at. A perfectly free and ignorant system of horse breeding amongst the class and throughout the districts in these kingdoms from which the vast majority of our general horses proceed. A stallion gaining custom from the popularity of an owner perfectly regardless of his own good or bad qualities. Fillies only preserved to the country that from some objectionable qualifications render them beneath the speculative notice of a foreign agent. For years, as I have before said, colonels of cavalry regiments, contractors, veterinary surgeons, and practical men, in newspaper columns, have been registering experiences tending to exhibit shortness of supply, and want of the "wear and tear" characteristics in our general horses of a former period. Notwithstanding which, yearly recurring and increasing evils are allowed—without any countervailing attempt of a national character—to sow the seeds of carelessness and ignorance, that gives in its own time a crop of disappointment, chagrin, alarm, and disgust. And why should this be? Is it because the general English public is less at home upon the subject of horses than upon almost any other? Ought not that to be the chief reason why those confided with the nation's interests should be the more punctiliously careful? We have not the excuse of want of alarming warnings, or practical examples, as to the huge preponderating power that such an arm as a powerful and efficiently-mounted cavalry gives. We know, too, from the Royal Commission enquiries what our cavalry state is at present, and what it promises to be in the future under the existing state of things. We learn that the Franco-Prussian war has caused the deportation of thousands of most objectionable mares from these kingdoms, chiefly from Ireland, our greatest nursery. Everything concurs in pointing to *the present* as an opportune period for making a national stand against the nation's insidious and parasitic foe, a foe bred of apathy and ignorance, and fostered in cruel carelessness and censurable folly. When, alongside such views, we glance at the effect of continental judgment, energy, enterprise, and gold upon their and this country's horses through our open marts and ports for years past, be assured the picture is both a sad and serious one for any patriotic Briton to contemplate. France and Germany have year by year for a long time taken a majority of the best half-bred mares, nay, all they could get! Those very mares that properly should have been the seed from which *our* cavalry *not theirs* should grow remounts.

We are now—it is a matter of general notoriety—dependent upon foreign breeders, and that, save for the importations from abroad that fill the high class horse-dealing stables, horses for the ordinary purposes of fashionable life *would not be forthcoming at any price.* Happily the enormous prices for high-class horses that scarcity has begot in this country, has violently assailed the English aristocracy in that most sensitive part of an Englishman's system—his "breeches pocket." This pull upon the exchequer and temper of some of our *magnates* will conduce to making our subject more weighty as being so purely personal; and it is to be hoped that the searching influence of depletion in the purse will stimulate to an exercise of patriotism that, no doubt, only slumbered with the great and enlightened; and having been once aroused will awaken to a vigorous existence. "Out of evil comes good," and, I think, we shall find a wholesome agitation before long in the senate house of England on this subject of short and inefficient supply of ENGLAND'S HORSES FOR PEACE AND WAR.

If such results, the recent Continental War will have in one respect done England good service, by having conduced to a state of things by the closing of Continental Ports that first led to the general knowledge of our home scarcity by stopping the annual, nay, weekly imports from abroad, for a time. Had those supplies continued unimpeded we might have gone on in general ignorance of our state till a time when the course that has been running its exhaustive way would have left us in a much worse state for regenerative efforts than we are now.

If, then, it can be incontestably deduced from evidence, too sadly incontrovertible, that a majority of our *pur sang* horses are painfully unstable, effete, and decrepit, happily, we can produce very superior examples of high class animals of the same *caste*—the best of this order—but removed by their super-excellence from the immediate channels of general utility; nevertheless, numbers of sound and suitable stallions that have failed in those qualifications of *speed*, that is now the *ne plus ultra* of the racing arena, may be annually culled from the training stables at the "back end" of the turf season, applicable in every particular for the purposes of regenerating and improving our general and war horses, but at no "screw prices."

We have only to be competent and careful in selection, and judicious in placing such stallions where a wide and fertile field for their services will be open. And thus, having so far conformed to the leading principle of "the universal mother," in her own domains, *by resorting for the benefit of posterity to the best males,* let us confidently rely for results upon the unerring accuracy and sufficiency of that omnipotent dispensation that cannot err, and to which we thus become disciples.

Much mischief as has befallen this the most noble of his brute servants, from man's folly and vain-glory in the prostitution to his pomps and vices of a glorious animal given for different purposes—that has been his greatest physical auxiliary in the march from barbarism to civilization—this return, at even the eleventh hour, to the exercise of wise natural laws in our equine economy will be, unquestionably, attended with most satisfactory benefits, for—

> "If Nature be driven out with proud disdain,
> The powerful goddess will return again;
> Return in triumph to deride
> The vain attempts of luxury and pride!"

If we acknowledge the national misfortune forced upon our appreciation by existing facts, and grant that we have the remedy to a frightful evil in our own hands, what are we going to do? How harmoniously the nervous and caustic suggestion of my gallant and able brother-in-arms, "Picador," in *Bell's Life*, and "Vieille Moustache," in *The Field*, harks in here; he writes on this subject in March, 1871:—"'If you want a thing well done,' said his Iron Grace, the late Duke of Wellington, 'do it yourself.' If the state desires a good supply of horses in time to come, it must 'set its shoulders to the wheel;' and while pessimists are lamenting the extinction of their favourite class of horse, and optimists building castles in the air and enunciating visionary schemes, which can never be realized, the state must work while others are writing or thinking. Then, and not till then, will it be in a fair way to render itself independent of foreign supply, or private enterprise at home."

Words of wisdom these. It is a state question, and is only susceptible of treatment through national legislation and aid. For, although in a wealthy country like this private enterprise may, nay! will answer to the demand for supply through advanced market quotations, I am, from out my practical experience, fully persuaded that though the number of our general horses will surely increase under the consequences from exceptional scarcity, nevertheless, private enterprise will never produce for general utility that class of sire which alone can improve the race of our general horses, and maintain them in high excellence, from the self-evident reason, that the emolument to be derived from public stallions of high character would not pay the outlay imperative upon their procuration and maintenance.

There is no getting away from this axiom, and whatever may be the course of the Government when called upon to legislate for a question that brooks no longer "shelving"— the better direction and promotion of the supply of ENGLAND'S HORSES FOR PEACE AND WAR—there is the *bete noir* no casuistry or sophistry can anyhow dispose of, nor can it be amply treated but by acceding to the plague spot, and adopting prompt and practical measures to neutralize its painfully suggestive consequences.

See we not our position? Do we not ponder with sad forebodings upon the evidences we have perused from sources that, alas! admit of no doubt? Are not the remarks we have read from Cavalry Colonels, Army Contractors, and others, alarmingly suggestive of possible retribution for a national crime? Yes, crime! War is a possible contingency for this great nation. Horses are required in war. We see from example of recent times what an immense power they are. Our Cavalry strength in re-mounts is incomplete, so with our Artillery. What are we to do? Why, make up for lost time and stupidity by energy, talent, and wisdom. Have we not sadly exemplified the parable of "The Unwise Virgins"? May not the time for preparation pass? the hour of necessity be at hand? and we too late for present emergency? but, happily, not so for future provision.

Except the country is satisfied to dispose of these considerations, and content to lose that safety and *prestige* which attaches to it, of possessing the best horses and best mounted cavalry in the world, some national effort must be made to alter the existing state of things regarding the falling away in numbers and quality of our re-mount and general horses. What so largely contributed to give Cromwell's Ironsides so brilliant a page in History? What rode our mounted soldiers in the days of Ligonier's black horse to glory and conquest? What carried our mail-clad warriors, "Scots' Greys," and poor Erin's "Green Horse," through the chosen and serried ranks of France's great hero to the crowning victory of Waterloo? What bore with the irresistible career of a swooping eagle "our Immortal Six Hundred" over the flower of Russia's chivalry and her barbarian hordes? Oh! it was our glorious British horses, fleet, powerful, and beautiful; true as hearts of oak, and trusty as the puissant and flashing steel of their hero riders. And, shall we lose them? Yes! England, with sorrow I write the appalling conviction, a continuance of the present system, or rather, no system, and they will be known only to posterity through history or by tradition, "vanished as a tale that was told."

CHAPTER X.

HAVING thus far treated of "ENGLAND'S HORSES FOR PEACE AND WAR," in the past, present, and future, I venture to carry out my efforts on the noble animals' part still further by submitting for public consideration what I diffidently, but with confidence, entitle :—

EUREKA!

THE POWERS OF THE HORSE.—THEIR TRUE SEAT.

IN order that we may best apply the animal powers of the horse, with least waste or diminution to the will of man, in draught or burthen, it is expedient that we should study his structure, and from careful examination, fix the *true seat* of his powers. For it becomes a leading principle in the matter, that without knowing where what we want lies, we cannot use it to advantage, for we know not how effectively to obtain and apply it; and that it is extremely important that we should know the seat of *that* from which we expect to accomplish our object; and which, I may add, if we look for anywhere else but where it is, we shall find ourselves involved in as great a waste of power as would befall the millwright, who should immerse his wheel in "back-water" on the one hand, or elevate it out of the action of the falling stream on the other. But, with respect to the whereabouts of that muscular energy, which is the only moving power applicable to our machinery, we find the most varied and conflicting opinions, in which, the only point of agreement seems to be, that the fore and hind legs share, if not divide, the locomotive power of quadrupedal progression. These differences must be reconciled, and Riding Masters must coincide in their views as to the seat of that energy it is their business to apply, before any uniformity of management will exist, or a full development of power be attained.

It is obvious that no one can expect to derive the most advantage from the horse's powers until he has obtained the knowledge of where the source of ability for progression is located. The engine driver can tell whence are derived those powers his skill and education have taught him to wield at will; the agents in putting into action for man's exigent service that electric power hitherto the prerogative of Omnipotence, can explain how it is generated and brought into active co-operation with their desires; no trade, occupation, or calling, that its votaries will not understand its principle and action, if we except "Horse Breaking;" and this business, unfortunately, as a general rule, will be found in the hands of those who tax to the uttermost a power concerning which they neither know whence it comes, nor how it operates; and besides, they, for the most part, indulge in a repulsive species of pretension, which has had the effect of bringing their most important and critical occupation into a disrepute it should not intrinsically merit.

The fundamental principle of the only practical and enlightened system is, that the propelling power of the horse resides in his hind quarters, and *there* chiefly in the haunches.

Perhaps there cannot be found a more ready means of illustrating this proposition than by recurring to the example of the human biped; the sources of man's propelling powers being situated in his lower limbs, whether he move in his natural and erect position, or whether we suppose him thrown upon all-fours. In the latter case, the arms being merely employed to sustain the weight of the incumbent figure, which the legs and thighs press forward; and the heavy structure of man and the horse being so analagous, that if that be true in the case of the assumed incumbent position of the one, it may reasonably be inferred that it is so in the natural position of the other.

Arguments from analogy, though instructive for illustration, are not sufficiently terse and powerful for the establishment of principles, and therefore attention to an illustration of a stricter kind, by which the supposition that the principle of the fore legs in nature's economy was for the purpose of acting as only props or supports, and not in aiding locomotion by propulsion, may be diligently demonstrated, is demanded.

All progressive motion in organized beings is produced by alternate contraction and extension of their propelling members, whether the instrument of motion be the wing of a bird, the tail or fin of a fish, the annular process of the reptile, or the leg of the biped or quadruped; its efficiency equally depends upon its being brought into contact with the resisting medium when in a state of contraction, so that the corresponding extension, where it takes place, necessarily forces the body forward in the direction of the least resistance. Thus, the bird and the fish cleave a passage through their media of air and water respectively, and so all creatures which move on the surface of the earth bring their propellers, or motive power, to the point of resistance from which they obtain a fulcrum in a contracted state, moving their weight forward with a velocity proportioned to the power exerted in the subsequent extension of the contracted members.

In the case of the sound horse, the fore leg comes to the ground in an extended state, all its bones, with the exception of those at the pastern joint, abutting on one another in very nearly a straight line, from the point of the shoulder to the extremity of the leg, so that being manifestly incapable of further extension, it must be concluded, on the principles just laid down, that it is incapable of exerting any propelling energy, and consequently the only purpose it can serve is that of sustaining the weight of the incumbent fore quarter during the successive advances of the hind legs in their office of propulsion. Add to this important consideration that the heavy structure of the fore legs is joined to the rest of the frame by merely muscular attachments, calculated not to communicate impulse, but to break concussion; and I trust it will appear that we have sufficient grounds for justifying the conclusion that the propelling of the horse does not reside in his fore legs.

But when we turn to the hind legs, which, instead of like the fore, being united by a flexible and elastic muscular attachment to the rest of the frame, are inserted into the extremity of the spinal column by connecting bones of large dimensions, and eminently calculated, from their direction, to communicate impulse to the whole figure, we find all the conditions requisite for the exertion of progressive energy present in a very high degree. The limb is brought to the ground with all its parts in a high state of contraction, the shank bone forming an angle with the upper leg bone, or *tibia*, at the hock; the *tibia* forming an angle with the thigh bone, or *femur*, at the stifle joint; and the *femur* forming again another angle with the haunch bone or *ischium*, which last abuts directly on the *lumbar vertebræ*, and is the immediate agent in conveying the impulse of the hind legs to that centre of the system. Here, then, we have a series of no less than three angles, not to speak of the elastic apparatus of the pastern, in the successive opening out of which, by contraction of the limb at every stride, all the muscular energy of the hind quarters is called into play, and thus the foot forming the point of resistance, the body of the animal at every stretch of the hind legs is shot forward with a velocity proportioned to the amount of muscular action exerted in that process of extension. Thus it becomes perfectly clear that the whole propelling power of the horse is situated in, and exercised by, the hind quarters.

CHAPTER XI.

LIMITS OF THE HORSE'S POWER—CENTRE OF GRAVITY.

HAVING fixed the seat of that power it is the business of the riding-master to apply to the most advantage, let us next endeavour to ascertain the limits to its operation. The utmost measure of extension of which the limb is capable, will evidently constitute the limit of this power on the one hand, and the utmost measure of contraction on the other.

The first hint may be easily fixed, depending, as it does, on the natural conformation of the limb. In most instances the greatest angle which the *femur* can form with the haunch bone is limited to about 130°; again, the *femur* and *tibia* joined at the stifle joint can rarely form an angle greater than 140°; and the *tibia* and shank bone joined at the hock open out to their fullest extent at from 150° to 165°, in proportion to the prominence of the *os calcis*. In these maximum amounts of opening, therefore, we have the limit of the animal's progressive energy on the side of extension; in the other direction they are not quite so easily ascertained.

It is obvious that if the joints of the limb were sufficiently flexible to admit of its being brought to the ground in that very high state of contraction in which the parts are almost in contact, we should have the muscular energy of which the parts are capable brought into play in their extension, and consequently would attain the highest velocity that such an apparatus is capable of communicating: but not only are the limbs of the horse incapable of this extreme degree of flexibility, but their measure of contraction is further limited by the disposition of the weight which they have to sustain as well as to propel, and the position of the superincumbent weight in the unburthened animal is the creature's own centre of gravity, being the point at which its entire weight is connected.

This point in the horse, according to the various proportions of the animal, is found more or less in advance of the flank, and commonly in the middle of the "false" or "back ribs." Now, it is plain that, in proportion as the hind leg is brought up in a higher state of contraction, the foot, which forms the point of resistance to the whole propelling apparatus, will be thrown to a corresponding extent further forward, and so, in an extreme case such as we have supposed, will come to the ground considerably in advance of the centre of gravity; but when this weight is thus disposed behind the point of resistance, the exertion of power is calculated rather *to lift* than to propel it, and consequently, if there were no other element to be taken into account in our calculations, we should conclude on this branch of the subject that the centre of gravity in the animal as he stands gave the limit of which we are in search; and when the animal is only beginning to progress, such is, in fact, the proper limit assigned to the advance of the hind foot, but so soon as motion commences, a new force comes into operation in the *momentum*, compounded of weight and velocity of the moving body, which of itself tends to carry the centre of gravity forward with an independent velocity, proportioned to the original speed by which it is generated.

In high speed, therefore, the point of support may be taken by the hind foot considerably in advance of where the stationary centre of gravity would be, since the weight is continually borne forward by a force, independent of that about to be exercised by the extending limb, and which suffices to carry it over and past the point of resistance, before each accession of muscular energy from the propelling members comes to bear upon it.

This force being in proportion to the velocity, it follows that the greater the speed the more contracted will be the condition of the hind leg in coming up to the proper point or resistance, and consequently the greater extent of ground covered at each stride; and as the velocity and stride are thus increased, the body, from the greater obliquity of its supporters, will approach nearer the earth; hence we see the racer, in full speed, skim along with his belly very contiguous to the ground, bringing up his hind legs at each stride, so as to catch the flying centre of gravity, by an effort which may be said to mark the utmost limit of their contractile exertion.

In the centre of gravity, therefore, whether stationary as in the horse trying to put himself in motion, or progressive, as when he is propelled both by *momentum* and by successive accessions of muscular energy from behind, we have the proper limit of contraction, of which we have been in search. So far, therefore, we conclude, 1st, that the propelling powers reside in the hind legs and haunches: 2nd, that these powers are in proportion to the amount of contraction and extension of which the parts are capable; and 3rd, that the limits within which they are exercised are the extremity of the outstretched limb, on the one hand, and the point immediately below the centre of gravity—stationary or progressive—on the other.

If by extravagant action those limits be overpassed in front, the consequence, as I have remarked, will be a certain degree of embarrassment, the point of resistance being in advance of the weight; if they be overpassed behind, injury to the hock or haunch will be the result of that excessive extension; but while straining and embarrassment thus attend on every excess of action beyond either limit, they will also attend, in a greater or less degree, on every falling short of the same bounds, though they will be chiefly in the case of *deficient contraction*.

Deficient contraction exists whenever the hind foot fails to overtake the advancing centre of gravity; the weight is then in advance of the point of resistance, and the horse, in urging it forward, labours under the same disadvantage as would be experienced by the man who should attempt to throw the heavy shoulder stone from a point in advance of his foot. Both cases fall under the conditions of the third order of lever where the power is applied between the *fulcrum* and the weight, and in which it is a well-known law of mechanics, that as the weight is advanced the power is diminished. So with the horse, whose hind foot is his fulcrum, and whose power is concentrated in his haunches, in proportion as his centre of gravity overshoots the point to which he brings up his hind foot at each stride, is the loss of power and corresponding strain upon the embarrassed members.

A familar example of the same principle is afforded by an ill-trimmed boat, when too much of her cargo is stowed in front, and she becomes, as it is termed, "down by the head." Her sailing powers are thus greatly diminished, and that pressure of the canvas, which, in a properly balanced state of the vessel, would be wholly exerted in carrying her forward, now exercises a considerable portion of her force in burying her bows under water; what the mainsail is to the cutter, the haunches are to the horse, and it may be justly said, put either "out of trim" and the more sail you carry the less progress you are likely to make.

CHAPTER XII.

THE CENTRE OF GRAVITY DISPLACED.—DISORGANIZATION.—THE CONSEQUENCE.

ALTHOUGH the principles arrived at by this train of reasoning are illustrated and realized in the figure of action of the wild horse of the Pampas, or of the desert, as we observe him pictured and described in works of travellers; and although in the figure and action of other quadrupeds, which have not been subjected to draught or burthen, such as the deer, the hare, the greyhound, we observe they all use the *fore legs* for the purposes of support only, and all in bringing up their propellers, overtake and support the centre of gravity, attaining so to that beautiful balance of the figure which gives such an air of grace and ease to their movements; yet, we rarely, if ever, find in the domesticated horse a single one of those characteristics of action, which such a distribution of his powers ought to produce. On the contrary, we find him in almost every case thrown more or less on his forelegs, not only for support, but for a false means of progression, to make up for the deficient exercise of his true propellers; and as the application of any instrument in the economy of nature to purposes for which it was not designed, it is necessarily punished with disease. We rarely, if ever, find him free from blemish, while in a majority of cases, defects, amounting almost to unsoundness, are repulsively visible, crippling his movements, shortening the period of his usefulness, and detracting from the pleasure and advantage of his owner.

It may at first sight appear strange, that these imperfections in carriage, with their attendant train of malformations and blemishes, should exist in the young animal as he is usually put into the hands of the trainer; but nothing is more certain than that peculiarities of gait and carriage are transmitted from one generation to another. The observant enquirer will be at a loss to account for the original introduction of those peculiarities, they being all owing to the mistaken manner in which the animal in his natural state has been subjected to the artificial duties of draught or burthen.

The wild horse, unaccustomed to either, moves, as do other quadrupeds, in their native state, in perfect balance; because at each stride he brings up his propellers to the point directly beneath his centre of gravity; but the moment he receives a rider or burthen, that centre is shifted forward; for, the seat which convenience most readily resorts to for the saddle back-band, or hooser, just behind the withers, and on which we impose all the burthens we lay upon the animal, is so situated that a heavy body placed there does not press over the point where the weight of the *unencumbered* animal is concentrated, but several inches in advance of it. The *new centre of gravity* of the whole mass is thus shifted forward to an intermediate point, more or less in advance of that to which the animal in his wild state had been accustomed, and beyond which natural requirement had not called upon him to bring up his motive powers. The consequence is, that his hind legs now act at a disadvantage, and the animal, to make up for their diminished deficiency, has recourse to his fore legs as instruments not only of support, but of progression.

This is the first fatal step; it leads directly to all the evils that usually beset this noble creature through man's careless ignorance. The fore legs having now assumed the office of auxiliary propellers, must, as we have already seen, come to the ground in a state of contraction, and as their structure precludes contraction at any joint except that of the knee, they now come to the ground with a bend at that joint, and are thus at once converted from the straight and firm supporters that nature made them, and which they were, or ought to have been, before the artificial change of the centre of gravity, into a pair of bent and tottering props, ready at the least trip or interruption to collapse beneath their burthen. Thus the direct and immediate consequence of the first false step is, that the horse becomes a stumbler, and is continually subject to the danger of breaking his own knees and his rider's neck. But further, the bending of the knee, however slight, shortens, more or less, the height of the support afforded to the fore quarter of the animal by the fore-leg; and it is a well-known fact, that if a weight be carried between two points, one of which is lower than the other, as if a hand-barrow be borne between a long and short man, the burthen falls more heavily upon the latter. But without that bending of the knee the animal is unable to compensate for the loss of power which he now experiences in his true propellers; the next step towards destruction which he therefore takes, is to make up for this loss of natural height in his anterior supporters, made necessary by that compensation for the loss of power in his hind legs to which I have just adverted, by straightening out his pasterns, and standing as it were *on his toes*. This restores the level, and relieves the fore legs from that increased burthen to which the bending of the knee had subjected them; but it *doubles* the risk of stumbling, and brings on directly every one of that multiplicity of diseases to which the fore-foot and leg are so notoriously subject.

For the pastern now, instead of discharging its natural office of an oblique spring interposed between the hoof and the rest of the limb for the prevention of excessive concussion, becomes a direct and rigid prolongation of the shank, and so communicates to the whole limb, and to that delicate plate of muscles which forms its only attachment to the rest of the frame, the shock of every stroke of the hoof against the ground. If we begin at the hoof, and trace the direct consequences upwards, we shall find first that the hoof, no longer resting flat on the ground, but bearing chiefly on the toe, becomes liable to contraction, both directly from the resistance of the iron shoe, and indirectly (which is the most frequent symptom) from internal inflammation resulting from the same cause; that the small bones of the foot, squeezed together by the weight resting directly on the extremity of the "coffin bone," are all in their turn liable to inflammation at their points of juncture, the navicular bone especially, which is so often the seat of the worst cases of lameness, that the deposit of bone being stimulated by the pressure and concussion to which all parts are thus exposed, the joints become liable to callosities and bony enlargements, which too frequently involve the whole foot in some of the worst species of unsoundness, in shape of ossified cartilages and ringbone.

Following the mischief up the leg, we next find the "back sinew," which Nature chiefly designed for the purpose of lifting the foot and contracting the pastern, deprived of all opportunity of exercising its proper functions, and so exposed to these enlargements consequent on that state of relaxation, so often mistaken for sprain in the back sinew.

Ascending higher, we find increased tendency to bony deposits, consequent on accumulated concussion of the parts, promoting the formation of large splints, which, though callous in themselves, almost invariably produces lameness when they are growing through the sensitive tissue, by irritating and pressing against the sheaths of the tendons which play over and beside them; and finally carrying our investigation to the upper extremity of the limb (with the cursory remark that this tendency to increased bony deposits, caused by accumulated concussion consequent upon the straightening out of the pastern joint, will appear in the bones of the arm and shoulder, as well as those of the foot and shank), we find the plate of muscles forming the attachment by which the blade bone is affixed to the trunk, suffering as well as the rest of the limb from the same evils; the shock of every stroke of the hoof against the ground, no longer broken by the elastic play of the pastern joint, being communicated directly to these fibres, which, not being designed in the structural economy of the animal for resisting such concussion, are often affected by inflammation and even rupture, producing the most serious cases of shoulder lameness.

But the evil does not rest here. This bending of the knee and straightening of the pastern necessarily throws the fore feet *backwards;* these now standing in the way of the hind feet, the latter, in sympathetic accommodation, also fall back from their true position, thus aggravating the evil already existing by throwing a still further burden upon the fore feet, which, again yielding to the increased bending of the knees and greater erectness of the pasterns, called for by the increasing necessity for finding some progressive power independent of the true propellers, creep back a little further, and push the hind feet more and more from their natural position, till the latter, no longer resting flat on the ground under an oblique pastern, but propped on the toes with the pastern extending similarly to the fore feet, become liable to similar evils, only that those bony deposits which are the invariable accompaniments of concussion, taking the form of splints on the shank bone of the fore leg, assume the more formidable character of "spavin" in the joint of the hock.

Such are the pains and penalties by which NATURE admonishes and afflicts for the abuse of any of her provisions—so "wise in their ends and economic in their means"—and as her arrangements have been systematically disregarded (time out of mind) by the manner in which we compel our beasts of burthen to conform to our impositions, it is not surprising that, with the addition of other concurrent abuses, they should be productive of evil consequences to the horse generally, and that he should have entailed upon him in the domestic state an inclination to a faulty carriage, and predisposition to, if not actual, disease, far too generally in very foalhood.

CHAPTER XIII.

THE CENTRE OF GRAVITY RESTORED—DISORGANIZATION PREVENTED.

It is palpable that all those evils would have been avoided if, in first subjugating the horse to his uses, man had either taken means to adapt the burthen to the figure of the animal, so as not to disturb the natural centre of gravity, in which case the horse would have preserved his balance without any alteration in extent of his action; or else before imposing the burthen, had trained the animal to a foreign and extended action, such as would compensate in the harmony of motion to the unnatural distribution of the weight to be carried; in which latter case the natural balance would be exchanged for an artificial one, but the animal machine would by factitious aid still move in equilibrium, and so escape the consequence of being thrown on other resourses for motion than on those which nature has provided.

It is equally obvious, now, that in seeking to restore the animal to a proper use of his powers, and to preserve him from innumerable ills that attend on the perversion of those purposes of nature which he has been made the victim and example of; it is open to the breaker either to exert his skill to bring the animal back to the natural balance of the wild horse, and then to impose his burthen in such a way as not to disturb that balance, or else to extend the natural action sufficiently to prepare him for the reception of a burthen imposed in the ordinary way.

That the former one would be the course more strictly congenial to the natural economy, I do not doubt, and that in not adopting it we expose ourselves to some bad consequences, I am well persuaded ; still the difficulty existing from structural inconvenience in the application of draught and burthen in any but the ordinary manner, and the immemorial adhesion of man to the long established mode of harnessing and saddling, render it almost impossible that it should get practically that preference to which in principle it is clearly entitled.

The only course, then, open to the breaker is the latter of the two above mentioned, it being efficacious not only for the full development of the powers of the animal, but also for complete prevention and even cure of those ailments which I have already enumerated.

The earlier after three years old that the horse for ordinary purposes of utility, fashion, or war, can be put into the hands of the riding master the better.

The cervical and dorsal vertebræ, which must in most cases receive a new direction, are after the age of three years comparatively stiff and settled in that false position to which I have adverted as being more or less entailed on the whole equine race in these countries. This hereditary assimilation to a deformity may be exemplified by an analagous misfortune to be found in the stooped shoulders, narrow chests, and shambling action of the majority of the population of crowded manufacturing towns : and as the drill sergeant, in forming recruits drawn from such districts for the reception of the knapsack, begins by forcing back the shoulders and elevating the head, so must the riding master, who would qualify the young horse for the reception of his rider or other burthen, commence his operations by a corresponding process of elevating this extremity of the spine ; not by the temporary and ruinous expedient of straightening out the limbs that support it, and thereby bringing on all the complicated ills which we have glanced at, but by a permanent alteration in the carriage of the animal's neck and shoulders, not to be effected without a corresponding improvement in the whole frame.

This alteration is effected by mechanical restraint, adapted to the varying figures submitted to it. The "ewe-neck," where, by elevating the head we depress the cervical vertebræ still further, will obviously require a different arrangement of the reins from that resorted to with the "rainbow," *i.e.*, arching-neck.

It would be beyond the purpose of this little manual to give any minute, and, possibly, too technical a description for general reading, of the apparatus to be employed ; suffice it to say, that a yoke or furniture having the property of adjustment suitable to every case can be conveniently fitted on any horse, and will have the effect, in a few lessons, more or less, according to age and formation of the animal, of forcing to raise the spine at the shoulder, being the process, in his case, corresponding to the forcing back of the spine at the same point in the human figure.

True it is, neither in the case of the biped, nor of the quadruped, can this alteration be effected without some degree of inconvenience, and even temporary pain ; but it would be as unreasonable to compromise the efficiency of our troops out of a mistaken sensibility for the sufferings of the recruit, as it is for some enthusiastic and mawkish people to sacrifice all hopes of rendering the horse permanently master of his educated powers, from their reluctance to subject him to temporary discipline.

Supposing the alteration, however, to be effected, the very first consequence of it will bring the riding-master into collision with another prevalent prejudice. It will readily be seen that in proportion as the shoulder is elevated, the weight is more thrown back upon the hind quarters, while the fore legs, being proportionately lifted from the ground, no longer have the same opportunity of catching or pushing at the surface that was afforded to them while the shoulder remained in its depressed condition. The consequence is, that the animal at once, and as a matter of necessity, begins to work his haunches with an energy proportioned to the increased demand upon them. But the very operation of putting the horse to the vigorous employment of his true instruments of progression, is unfortunately met at the outset by a prevailing idea, that putting the horse on his haunches, or "uniting him" as it is technically termed, is attended with bad consequences to the *hock*. To this it may be a sufficient answer to say simply, that nature, having designed the haunches as the true seat of the animal's progressive power, would never allow their legitimate use to be attended with bad consequences of any kind, either to themselves or to the neighbouring parts of the limbs; for disease is not normal, but acquired, being only the result of disorganization, and the invariable attendant of *abuse*, but never of the *due use* of any of *nature's* provisions; but however strongly the case may appear to have been made for the application of that argument, it may be well to meet the objection upon different and independent grounds:—and first, the true cause of hock ailments is not the excess, but the defect of action in the haunches, for then the hocks have to do the work the haunches have left undone, and the haunches have their work undone for this simple reason, that if they opened out and closed up to their full extent at every stride, the hind foot must needs come forward to a place where the fore foot stands in its way and impedes it; and the fore foot stands there, because the bent knee and straightened pastern have thrown it back from its proper place under the point of the shoulder; and the knee has been bent, and the pastern has been straightened, because the shoulder has, from time out of mind, been depressed by the imposition of burthens in advance of the point to which the animal has been taught to bring up his propellers; so that by elevating the fore hand, getting the fore feet out of the way, and putting the horse on his haunches, we not only do not throw any additional strain upon the hocks, but really relieve them of an undue task, which we thus confer and confine to the proper instruments provided by nature for its due performance.

And although apart from the subject with which I am here occupied, I ask pardon for digressing so far as to direct the mind of the reader to the adoption of this theory in confutation of the shallow and unreasoning objections so pathetically urged against the use of the bearing rein, which may be regarded in its judicious application as one of the *most humane* and excellent instruments known for the increased accession of the harness horse's powers in full vigour to the fulfilment of his tasks, and the preservation of his soundness.

To return to our subject, this operation of "uniting" the horse, which, under that name, is so much reprobated, is not only not condemned, but highly approved when it shows itself under any other name, and in consequences affecting another part of the body.

Everyone knows how much "a good mouth," as it is called, is justly prized amongst all lovers of the horse. "Does he ride to a good mouth?" is more frequently than any other the question of a high-class dealer in horses. In Ireland it is said, as one of the most attractive commendations that can be bestowed, that such a horse is "well snaffled." The terms are synonymous, and mean that he is light on hand, perfect in his paces, and so forth; and yet, if the matter be looked into, it will be found that the quality so much commended does not reside in the mouth at all, for, so far as mere organization is concerned, the mouths of all horses are as nearly as possible alike, and if the jaws of the hardest-mouthed "borer" in the world were submitted to the anatomist, side by side with those of the best broken and lightest-mouthed horse, it would be impossible for him to tell which was which, unless, indeed, from the greater tenderness of the "hard mouthed" one, caused by the merciless pulling which is ignorantly supposed callousness to the bit too frequently encourages. For this idea of some mouths being "calloused" is a mere vulgar prejudice, caused from the fact of hard pulling resulting from causes quite independent of the mouth. The mouth of every horse is exquisitely sensitive; the only callousness in the business is in the feelings of the rider, or rather, let me say, in his judgment, for if that were as sensitive to the facts before his eyes as the "bars" of the horse's mouth are to the bit with which he lacerates them, he would perceive that his horse leans on his hand, for support, not because he, poor beast, does not feel the inconvenience, but because *he cannot help it!*

It is *support* the "hard mouthed" horse looks for, in nine cases out of ten, and he is driven to seek that support where he can find it; and the reason why he needs it is simply this, that his forehand has fallen below its proper limit in the scale of a just balance, and so has to support an undue share both of his own weight and that of his rider. The consequence is, as has been already shown, that his fore legs fall back, and in their turn force back the propellers; the haunch no longer works through the whole of its proper space of action, for it cannot close completely up without bringing the propellers fully forward, and they, as we have seen, cannot get fully forward on account of the impediment offered by the displacement of the fore feet, which, in their turn, are equally unable to recover their proper position, while the shoulder continues depressed; the drooping head must be supported, no matter at what cost of pain to the "bars" of the poor animal's mouth. But raise the shoulder, get the fore feet out of the way, set the haunch to work, in other words, "unite" your horse and bring up his propellers, and you at once find his balance restored, his action extended, his *speed* and *strength* sometimes nearly doubled, and his head, which used to hang with so irksome a weight upon the arm of his rider, erect, free, light upon the hand, and perfectly sensitive to every admonition of the bit.

Such, in at least nine cases out of ten, is the true explanation and cure for the so-called "hard-mouth," as well as of the "uneven mouth," so termed when the horse pulls by one side of his mouth and moves obliquely. In the remaining cases, the cause is usually to be found in some malformation or acquired distortion of the vertebræ of the neck, causing the head to incline to a particular side, and so offering an obstinate resistance to the rein, which pulls in an opposite direction. Putting the horse on his haunches will not, it is true, cure this defect; but if the animal be not in balance, it will facilitate the cure, by leaving the head and neck free to the unimpeded operation of such other remedies as the skill of the breaker may enable him to adapt to the varying circumstances of each case.

To elevate the anterior extremity of the spine, then, with a view to restoring the animal to a proper state of balance, is the object of the first lesson given in this system of training; and, as observed, that object is attainable by different means, suitable to the varieties of form, habit, and temper exhibited by the horses placed in the breaker's hands.

If I be right in these views, founded as they are on the first principles of mechanical philosophy, it would follow that for contracted hoofs, ring-bone, navicular disease, splents, spavins, curbs, shoulder lameness, and all the rest of the organic diseases which affect horses, as well as in those supposed cases of lameness which are only the results from irregular and unbalanced action, the enlightened riding master should be applied to and not the veterinary surgeon; for the former can remove the original cause of the evil, the latter only prescribe for the effects from it.

ON THE SADDLE.

To attain to such a seat as will secure equilibrium and thus afford personal ease and comfort and facility for command over the horse, ought to be the first object of the tyro; and the formation of it will be rendered easier by attention to some very simple elementary considerations.

It is one of the rudimental laws of gravitation, that if any body, such as the person of a rider on horse-back, overhang the base on which it is supported, it will have a tendency to fall over, which can only be counteracted by external force, or by the exertion of muscular tenacity.

Now, the base on which the person of the horseman is supported, is, alternately, the saddle and the stirrups; it follows, therefore, that the rider will have a tendency to fall off, whenever his person is not directly over its point of support, on the saddle or in the stirrups, as the case may be; and this tendency he can only counteract by adequate muscular exertion.

But as all his muscular force (independent of the awkwardness and fatigue attendant on such continued exertion) ought to be employed in the control of his horse, or in such other exigencies as may arise, it becomes desirable, in the first place, that he shall attain to such a seat as will keep his centre of gravity directly over the base on which it is for the given moment of time supported. But, as I have mentioned, it is so supported from two points alternately—the saddle and stirrups. Consequently, if these two points be not in the same vertical line, the rider, to avoid falling off, will be obliged to shift his position at each motion of the horse, so as to bring his centre of gravity alternately over each; and in fact this is the method of riding which we every day witness in the field, the park, and streets, where the tuition of the efficient riding master has never been resorted to. In trotting, the uncultivated horseman is specially observable; where we see three out of four of our ordinary horsemen "jogging along," in a series of these awkward movements, rendered necessary by their having their feet far in advance of their seat on the saddle, so that at each vertical motion of the horse (which the good rider avoids by rising from the saddle and pressing the stirrups) they are obliged to shift the body to a corresponding extent; thus not only altering their own centre of gravity, at the cost of much tiresome and unseemly exertion, but, what is worse, breaking up and confusing the action of the best paced horse by continually shifting the weight he has to carry: a process which, I need hardly say, alters and shifts the centre of gravity of the whole mass, and consequently leaves the best trained animal uncertain how far to bring up his propellers, on which depends unity and harmony of action. With such a seat, the strongest man will be comparatively powerless in the saddle, and the most distinguished figure look mean and constrained. The repose so essential to a dignified carriage cannot consist with these hurried, anxious, and irregular movements; the steadiness of hand requisite for the support and control of the animal, and, without which, both horse and rider are in constant danger of coming to the ground, is wholly unattainable, and the sense of insecurity, combined with conscious awkwardness, renders the ride itself a species of irksome probation, rather than a delightful and exhilarating exercise.

But when the stirrup is brought perpendicularly under the saddle, then both points of support are on a line with the centre of gravity at the same time, and, consequently, one uniform position keeps the body of the rider over both, as each in succession becomes the point of support.

This seat once attained by practice, the rider will himself be in balance, no matter where the saddle may be placed, for the seat will always be under the shoulder, and the stirrups under the seat.

But the tyro must not expect that the ordinary announcements of "riding taught in six lessons" will ever accomplish anything for him beyond the creation of a conviction that at the expiration of his half-dozen experiences he has just learned enough to convince that he knows nothing but of the most rudimental character. Six months' careful attendance with such a man as "Fred Allen," would, no doubt, suffice to turn out a "finished horseman."

To complete the equilibrium of horse and rider, it will be necessary to regulate the position of the saddle, so that when the rider occupies his seat, the additional weight may either coincide with the centre of gravity of the horse (which would be perfection of balance), or, where that is possible, that it may, at all events, lie within the limits of such action as the animal has been trained to.

Then the complete balance is established; the horse moves with the same freedom as in his native pastures, the only difference being that his weight has been increased by the imposition of a load, which his habitual action is competent to sustain and propel, and which he finds precisely where custom has brought his limbs to expect it; while the load itself—neither lying a dull weight, like an inanimate burthen, nor jerking backward and forward, like an unskilful horseman—accommodates itself by an easy and spontaneous movement to every motion of the horse, affording at the same time support, guidance, and encouragement; in a word, endowing the energies of the brute with a portion, as it were, of the rider's reason.

If the seat so gained were found inferior to other more easily attained postures, in any of the requisites for perfect horsemanship; if in that position, for instance, the hand of the rider were less able to compete with the pull of the reins; or if in the leap his person were more exposed to the tilt of the hind quarters, and so his seat less secure, then it might be doubted whether it were worth while, for the preservation of a perfect balance, to subject the rider to these inconveniences. But as it always happens where a true principle is the foundation of our reasoning, whatever is pointed out by that principle will be found consistent with everything else that properly connects itself with the subject; so here we find the seat indicated by the necessity of balance to be that in which all the powers of man and horse act together with the greatest amount of ease and efficiency in the performance of everything that appertains to perfect horsemanship.

At first sight, it might appear as if those postures which pupils in riding schools, or elsewhere, are prone to assume, from the analogy that naturally suggests itself between sitting upon an ordinary seat and upon a saddle, and in which the legs are stretched forward in an extended state, with the stirrups pushed up towards the horse's shoulders, would afford the means of offering the most resistance to the pull of the reins, however awkward and insecure it might be in other respects; for here the resistance from the stirrups is nearly on a line with the direction of the pull, while in the perpendicular posture it is nearly at right angles to it. But when we consider that action and reaction are equal and opposite, we shall easily perceive that any oblique action on the stirrups, communicating its reaction through the outstretched limbs, has a direct tendency to tilt the figure back upon the saddle, in a direction which neither gravitation nor muscular action can oppose; so that before the rider can avail himself of the resistance of his foot in such a position, he may be said to have already lost his seat.

But the perpendicular position of the vertical reaction of the stirrup, supposing it to be communicated in full force to the person, is directly met by the downward pressure of the rider's weight, and this alone is sufficient to reinstate the figure in its proper position. But that upward tilt, even before it comes into opposition to the gravity of the body, is broken and carried off by the spring of the knee, at which there must necessarily be a slight angle, to bring the foot back to its position under the seat; so that in the perpendicular position the whole weight and muscular pressure of the rider descend upon the seat and stirrups without any counteracting influence whatever. The more the rider in such a position presses the stirrups, the lighter will be the grasp which his thighs will take of the saddle, and the more immovable the resistance which his trunk will offer to the pull of the reins.

On the contrary, in the oblique position, every pressure of the foot will re-act against the trunk, because it will neither be broken by spring at the knee (the leg in that position being necessarily extended), nor opposed by the vertical force of gravitation, and will consequently detach not only the seat, but the thighs themselves from the saddle.

To pull such a rider out of the saddle the run-away horse will only have to overcome a resistance equal to the difference between the rider's weight and the pressure on the stirrups; so that the more he presses on the stirrups, the lighter he will be to lift.

To pull the *balanced rider* from his seat, not only must his entire muscular power be overcome, but *his entire weight must be lifted vertically out of the saddle!* and that, by a force acting at right angles to his figure, which is practically impossible.

So also the perpendicular, or military seat, is found the most convenient for avoiding those shocks, which are inseparable from high action. It is impossible to bring the figure into this position without making such an arrangement of the limbs, from the hip downwards, as brings the flat of the thigh in immediate contact with the saddle, with the back of the limb turned outward; in which position it is evident that the immediate line of contact at the seat must be limited to a very small portion of the person, and that directly under the weight. A vertical shock striking the rider there, may lift him vertically, but his position will be immediately restored by the counteracting influence of gravity; and if the shocks be of a peculiarly violent nature, it may be avoided altogether by detaching that portion of the seat from the saddle, which the command of the stirrup enables at all times the rider in our day to effect, without in the least degree interfering with the main line of attachment to the saddle, extending down the entire length of the limb. By the simple movement above described, the balanced horseman sails erect over the highest leaps in an easy curve, corresponding with that described by his horse's centre of gravity, to which his knees and thighs attach him, but wholly unaffected by the violent motion of the hind quarters, out of the influence of which he has thus raised the only portion of his person liable to such disturbance.

On the contrary, the oblique seat exposes the rider at every leap, and indeed at every pace, to a tilt from behind, which he can only avoid by the awkward expedient of throwing his trunk and shoulders so far back as to shift his seat forward out of the way of the visitation; a sudden *grip* with the calves of his legs being the only substitute left for the proper attachment of the thighs, which is necessarily broken up and neutralized by the movement.

It is true this seat of balance is not to be obtained but by pains and practice. The sitting posture, to which we are habituated, inclines the limbs to a wholly different arrangement from that to which we must conform them in the saddle; the hips and haunches, not so much used in other exercises, must be handy, flexible, and obedient; the feet must be used in a posture directly opposite to that taught by the dancing-master. Presence of mind, so little called for in ordinary walks of life (but which is in itself a necessary attendant on the position of equilibrium), must be cultivated and established; a daring confidence in the power of balance to carry the rider through anything, and over anything, that his horse can pass, must be so implanted in the mind, and become the fundamental principle of the pupil, to such an extent, that there will be no room for hesitation or doubt, should a moment of difficulty arise. In a word, the rider, as well as the horse, must go through his proper course of training; or that of the animal, in the first instance, will have been of no avail.

Is it not strange that with so many difficulties on every hand, with so much to be acquired, and so much to be forgotten, horsemanship, of all the other exercises to make a fully accomplished person, is the only one for which there is a great laxity and carelessness in seeking the best master?

We should justly call the young person a simpleton, who would stand up in a crowded ball-room without having received a lesson in dancing; who would attempt a duet, while ignorant of the gamut; or who would fight a duel with rapiers, never having so much as handled a foil. But that bug-bear to advancement, custom, has reconciled us, amongst other monstrosities, to the sight of hundreds of aspirants to horsemanship, who do not hesitate to vault into the saddle without a single preliminary lesson, there coolly, and as a matter of course, to perpetuate such blunders, and exhibit such awkwardness, as, if they occurred in a quadrille or other dance, would cover the transgressor with confusion.

But to those who, regarding horsemanship as an accomplishment of the most important consideration in society, and for personal comfort and safety, set themselves to learn it, like any other branch of a complete education, the toil and pains of learning are amply repaid by very great pleasure, opportunities, and advantages.

If the educated horseman be fortunate enough to possess a well-trained horse, he keeps him so; if he mount an animal whose balance is defective, he soon discovers the defect, and removes it; every ride to such a horseman, or horsewoman, is an exercise of mind as well as body, and redounds to their profit, not only in point of recreation and health, but also in a positive addition to the value of the animal beneath him.

In the Hunt or Steeple-chase, while others, mounted, perhaps, on higher-bred and better horses, may be seen leaping short, or "running baulks," at every fence, their horses being in that state of extension which renders them incapable of collecting themselves for a well-measured or fearless spring; the educated rider will be observed, even on an inferior animal, timing his stride, and uniting him in such a way, as to bring him up to every fence with his propellers directly under his weight, and ready at the shortest notice to throw their whole energy into the leap, which accordingly is rarely unsuccessful; for it is a very wretched quadruped, indeed, that does not possess force enough, if properly husbanded and directed, to carry eleven or twelve stone over any ordinary hunting fence, though such fence may not unfrequently be seen to stop a clever hunter, when brought to the leap in an animated state, and his propellers insufficiently advanced. Many sad accidents I have seen to man and horse from this cause. I once saw in one day's steeple-chasing, the death of five beautiful animals from jumping short. All came to the point for taking off in an extended and uncollected state (for a horse may be extended and held well in balance at the same time); so that the spring being, necessarily, more from the shoulders than from the haunches, and consequently insufficient to propel the weight through a wide enough space, caused them to fail in clearing the fence they were endeavouring to negotiate.

The united state is that in which only the horse can be said to be fully amenable to the control of the reins. The run-away horse, as if conscious of the fact, invariably gets up his back, and throws himself on his shoulders when breaking away, and in such position it requires no inconsiderable skill nor slight exertion of power to pull the animal up; for the vertebræ of the neck are, in such cases, stretched out very nearly in the same line with the pull of the reins, and the fore hand cannot be got up, nor the pace moderated, till the reins can be got to act on these vertebræ like a bowstring, which in that position is sometimes very difficult to effect. But the fleetest and most spirited horse, if in balance, will be free from this vice; for the pull of a child's hand on the reins in such a state of carriage tells more on the figure of the animal than that of the strongest man against the outstretched neck of the "borer," so that to the other advantages I have enumerated as flowing from the system of tuition to horse and rider that I advocate, I may justly add that of greatly increased safety to the weak or timid, as well as increased ease, comfort, and satisfaction to all.

After my observations on the improved carriage of the horse, I proceed to give my views as to what, it strikes me, are the advantages derivable to the rider from instruction based on the same principles; for the same system which expands and disembarrasses the chest of the horse, by bringing his centre of gravity over its proper point of support, applies with equal force to the mounted equestrian of either sex.

To attain the "seat of balance," the rider, whether male or female, must throw back the upper part of the person, so as to bring the weight directly over the saddle, this arrangement of the figure is necessarily accompanied by a hollowing of the spine at the waist, the effect of which, coupled with the retraction of the head and shoulders, is to expand the chest to its full limits. And as the blood is vitalized by the influence of atmospheric air in the lungs, and the amount of energy required at each inspiration depends upon the extent of the lungs engaged in this process, it follows that the extension of the chest, especially when we are borne rapidly through fresh and pure air, is a certain means of giving increased vigour to all the vital functions; and I may add, that wherever healthy action is so induced, exhilaration of mind is its inseparable attendant.

This is a fact well worth the serious attention of parents and those having charge of youth.

It is well known, and every head of a family must have observed, that young persons of both sexes, but especially lads who are passing out of the age of boyhood, are frequently affected with dulness of spirits, in some instances amounting to dangerous melancholy. It is not for me to speculate upon the causes that too frequently convert the laughing boy into a morose youth, further than to say, that about this period of life there appears to be an increased demand for vital energy, while as yet the puerile lungs are not of sufficient capacity to admit, in this normal condition, a competent supply of vitalising air:—under such circumstances out-door exercise, of an exhilarating kind, is the natural and ready remedy. Walking may contribute towards the purpose to a certain extent; but after a moderate amount of exercise in that way, the increased action of the lower limbs exhausts all the acquired energy from the freer use of the lungs, and the body is not left any overplus of animation to impart to the mind. But in riding, where the limbs are comparatively at rest, this exhausting demand does not exist, and the mind at once partakes of increased animation of the body. "Taking fresh air" in an open carriage might at first sight appear equally beneficial; but the sitting posture as usually adopted is that of the contracted chest. To the extent only of breathing purer air is it an advantage, but, where the patient who would breathe *purer air, and more of it*, can bear the slight additional exertion of riding on horse-back, *the saddle is, unquestionably and emphatically, the seat of health and happiness;* and, to conclude these observations with an application of the subject with which they have been chiefly occupied, I will add, that the fatigues or dangers of the saddle will be more or less, very great or utterly insignificant, just in proportion as the horse and rider are in defective or in proper *balance*.

Such are the principles which every competent and reasoning judge of the subject will, I think subscribe to: and thus it is that I advocate the handling and riding of ENGLAND'S HORSES FOR PEACE AND WAR.

⁎ *Lessons for Ladies will appear in a future edition that has been called for.*

UNDER ROYAL PATRONAGE.

CAPTAIN DE VERE HUNT'S HORSE AGENCY.

ESTABLISHED NEARLY 20 YEARS.

Under the patronage of nearly all the Royal Courts and a majority of the noble families and aristocracy of Europe.

Vide Testimonials below.

VERE D. DE VERE HUNT,

PROPRIETOR OF

THE OLD ESTABLISHED AND HIGHLY PATRONIZED HORSE AGENCY.

(Verbum sat Sapienti)!

HORSES OF EVERY DENOMINATION FOR HOME USE AND EXPORTATION.

THOROUGHBRED STALLIONS:—Selected carefully for transmission of desirable qualities to progeny.
BROOD MARES:—With length, room, blood, quality, bone, and action.
RACE HORSES:—In training, promising, or of public repute.
STEEPLE CHASERS:—"Dark," or in training, with established character.
MATCHED PAIRS:—Of every colour and kind, from the lady's blood Galloways to 17 hands high state horses.
LADIES' HORSES:—My specialité!!!
HUNTERS:—Up to all weights, and suitable to all purses!
OFFICERS' CHARGERS:—Suitable for, or steady with troops.
HEAVY-WEIGHT COBS:—With appearance and manners.
LIGHT-WEIGHT COBS:—With character, action, and manners.
CHILDREN'S PONIES:—Broken and steady, or otherwise to order.
MATCH TROTTERS:—Foreign and English.
BROUGHAM HORSES:—From 100 to 400 guineas.

At this exceptionally scarce and dear season in the home market this well-known Agency will be found of incalculable benefit to purchasers of horses for any purpose of saddle, harness, the turf, or stud, from the widely known exclusive advantages and opportunities at disposal of the proprietor.

VERE D. DE VERE HUNT,
Author of "The Horse and his Master," [Longmans], "England's Horses for Peace and War," &c., &c. [Bemrose], "Shamrock," and "North Tipperary," in *Bell's Life*, &c., &c.

Founder and proprietor of The Royal British and Foreign Horse Registry. The recognised and valued medium of the Courts and Aristocracy of Europe and the East.

N.B.—Testimonials from royalty, nobility, gentry, military and naval officers, clergymen, and professionals of the very highest order will be forwarded free to any address. Personal references to clients at home and abroad.

Address by letter for particulars or appointment, Captain DE VERE HUNT, Boscobel House, Regent's Park, London, N.W. Established nearly 20 years.

[See over for Testimonials, &c.

Some of many letters in testimony of the Proprietor's *efficiency* and *trustworthiness* as an AGENT FOR SALE AND PURCHASE OF HORSES.

From LORD COWLEY, *British Ambassador at Paris.*

Chantilly, Oise,
August, 1861.

To CAPTAIN DE VERE HUNT,
Royal British and Foreign Horse Registry, London.

SIR,—The certificates of the horses selected by you for me are quite satisfactory, except that the bay is not quite five years old, which to my mind, diminishes its value. I want you now to purchase for me a pony, 13—2 high, bay if possible, and quiet in harness; he must be a fine and free goer, and high-class, like my other horses. Answer me to this place, if you please. I testify to your zeal in my commission.

I am, Sir,
Your obedient servant,
COWLEY.

From THE COUNT FLEURY, *Consul-General of France, Queen's Gardens, Bayswater.*

SIR,—I have written to inform my brother, GENERAL FLEURY, of the charger you have selected for THE EMPEROR, and you will now receive your further orders from Head Quarters.
Thanking you for your satisfactory exertions in the matter,
I am, with consideration, &c.,
JULES FLEURY, *Consul-General.*
To CAPT. HUNT.

From the same.

SIR,—I have inspected the pair of driving ponies you have selected for Her Imperial Majesty the Empress. They are as beautiful animals and as well matched as I have seen, but alas! too small. I am more sorry than you can be for this, as I know well the difficulty of getting such pictured beauties. Persevere, and name your own terms if successful.

I have the honour, with consideration, &c.,
JULES FLEURY.
To CAPT. HUNT.

From THE HON. COLONEL MAUDE, *First Equerry to Her Majesty Queen Victoria.*

Royal Stables, Buckingham Palace,
June, 1871.

SIR,—I tried the phæton horses you brought me yesterday, and if you call here you will be paid for them.
I shall be pleased to see any horses you select for the Royal Stud. I want hacks particularly just now, such as I described to you.

Your obedient servant,
C. MAUDE.

From THE COUNT DE CYGALY, "*Master of the Horse*" *to the King of Italy.*

Turin,
April 22nd, 1861.

SIR,—By His Majesty's order, I immediately answer your letter about the bay and chestnut (thorough-breds) you have selected for His Majesty.
I must still make a few observations respecting these horses. It is necessary, I shall repeat, that they must not exceed 15 hands high, must be perfectly sound, without any defect in the legs, especially that the tendons have

not been injured in any way, as they are destined for parade horses for the King. Their age must not exceed seven years.

If in these respects they please your judgment, you are requested to despatch them immediately, by the usual route, to the Royal Stables here.

I beg you to advance the Groom £50 as the necessary expenses of the journey. The £500 for the horses and the £50 will be paid immediately to your order by Mr. Heath, His Majesty's Consul in London.

I remain, Sir, yours, &c.,
V. DE CYGALY, *Master of the Horse.*

From THE RIGHT HON. LORD GIFFORD, *Twenty Years a Master of Fox-Hounds.*

Ampney Park, Cirencester,
September 5th, 1861.

CAPTAIN HUNT,—I beg to enclose you a cheque for the little Arab; he is worth fifty of the grey I bought myself, and carries Lady Gifford most beautifully. I rode him cub-hunting with Mr. Greaves, and he is as active as a cat, and can put a leg anywhere.

After a long experience in horse matters, I must say, I have never known an instance where strict adherence to my directions, and skill and judgment were more satisfactorily displayed than in your recent selection for me. And I am much pleased with your energy, capacity, and liberality in the business between us; and shall never fail to give you a "good turn," when opportunity offers, amongst my friends.

Yours,
GIFFORD.

From THE RIGHT HON. LORD LLANOVER.

Monday Morning.

DEAR SIR,—I rode the hack you selected for me on Saturday, and like him sufficiently well to negotiate further as to price, which you must abate a little if you mean to deal with me.

I have sent you a friend for carriage horses—take care of him, he is no judge himself.

Yours obediently,
LLANOVER.

From THE RIGHT HON. LORD PALMERSTON.

Cambridge House, Piccadilly,
Thursday Morning.

CAPTAIN DE VERE HUNT,—I called upon you yesterday about "Baldwin." You have been prompt and expeditious in the matter, and I am sorry I cannot accept the offer made by Mr. Holmes. If he will allow you to advance, see me on the subject.

Yours, &c.,
PALMERSTON.

From MR. LONGFIELD.

Castle Mary,
Co. Cork.

To CAPTAIN DE VERE HUNT,

MY DEAR SIR,—I have received your letter offering me £10,000 for " Caroline," " Blarney," and " Union Jack." His Lordship's offer, through you, is liberal; but the fact is, I breed and race for my own amusement, and being easy on the score of money, I beg, with thanks, to decline.

Hoping to see you at Newmarket,

I remain, yours truly,
W. LONGFIELD.

From the HON. COLONEL CHOLMONDLEY, *Abbott's Moss, Northwich, Cheshire.*

Abbott's Moss.

DEAR SIR,—I have great pleasure in stating, that in all my transactions with you (and I have entrusted valuable horses with you to dispose of for me, as well as having bought and exchanged through your agency), I have always found you most competent, anxious to please by any means in your power, and furnishing good horses; and always ready to assist upon equitable terms an exchange, if such was desirable from any cause, such as a horse not suiting in the most trivial way, and I have known you most zealous for others in the exercise of your "calling."

Yours truly,
THOMAS CHOLMONDLEY.

From REAR-ADMIRAL RUSSELL ELLIOTT, *Appleby Castle Stud Farm.*

DEAR SIR,—I am sorry to hear you contemplate some change in your present mode of carrying on business as a COMMISSION AGENT FOR THE SALE OF HORSES.

For, as an extensive breeder of general horses, I have found your skill, your judgment, and your zeal very useful in disposal of my stock, after they had been broken and put in condition; and the general public well understand the value of an agency through which the usual trouble and risk is completely and satisfactorily dispensed with. While more *horsey* people, I know, regarded the practical trials you can make, the inquiries your experience and facilities can institute, and the species of shield at your disposal, as desirable adjuncts not attainable except through your agency.

I am, your obedient servant,
RUSSELL ELLIOTT, *Rear-Admiral.*

From the REV CANON PROTHERO, *Chaplain to the Queen.*

Whippingham,
East Cowes, 1869.

MY DEAR SIR,—I am much obliged to you for your active and satisfactory exertions on my behalf; you have supplied me with a pair of horses, and did it with less trouble and expense than I could myself accomplish. I am well pleased with your kind and active efforts.

Very truly yours,
GEORGE PROTHERO.

From W. H. BAINBRIGG, *Woodseat, Ashbourne, Derby.*

MY DEAR SIR,—My dealings with you have been of a most satisfactory character. I have sold valuable horses through your efficient and highly desirable agency.

I have recently received a letter from Mr. Sitwell, the Master of the Ludlow Hounds, in which he writes respecting the horse you selected from my stud for him; "I like him very much indeed, and consider him very clever at any kind of fence."

This is another tribute to your sound judgment of a hunter, as I tried hard, I confess, to sell you any of my others in preference.

I have found you strictly straightforward and *above board* in all I have had to do with you, and *cautious* as a Red Indian.

Yours faithfully,
W. H. BAINBRIGG.

*From the Owner of "*THE LAMB,*" the dual Winner of the Liverpool Steeplechases.*

BY SPECIAL APPOINTMENT.
Veterinary Surgeon to His Excellency the Lord Lieutenant.

16, Westland Row,
Dublin.

MY DEAR CAPTAIN,—In reply to your note, I beg to state, that during the course of a lengthened and extensive practice, which has thrown me amongst many of the greatest racing and hunting celebrities, I have met with *nobody* whose minute and practical judgment in *equine* affairs, and in the choice of valuable horses for any purpose, can surpass your own; and if I knew how to write my opinion of you on the subject in more forcible terms, I would feel myself justified in doing so.

I am, my dear Sir,
Yours very respectfully,
JOSEPH DOYLE, M.R.C.V.S.

Veterinary Establishment,
Waterford.

To CAPTAIN DE VERE HUNT,

MY DEAR SIR,—In reply to your note of the 3rd instant, I am very happy to add my affirmation to press and public award. I beg to state I can cheerfully bear testimony as to the very ample qualifications possessed by you in choice of horses. For I have had opportunities of testing your superior judgment in such matters, and in choice of valuable horses for varied purposes. I am quite sure my countrymen across the Channel will duly appreciate the value of such an agency as yours, in such able hands.

I am, my dear Sir,
Yours faithfully,
R. H. DYER, M.R.C.V.S.L.

From CAPTAIN KERR, V.C.

Sattara, Bombay Presidency, India,
October 14th, 1861.

SIR,—I want to employ you in a critical commission, which, from your writings, and the private recommendations I hold concerning you, I confess to placing in your hands with complete confidence.

I want a thorough-bred race-horse, a good one; very handsome, very sound, and very fast. He must have wonderful legs and feet to stand the wear and tear of our adamantine course and training grounds.

W H. KERR,
Maharratta Irregular Cavalry.

Albion Tower, Upper Norwood.

MY DEAR CAPTAIN HUNT,—As I leave for Bombay early in November, I wish you to procure for me the two other horses I require for racing in India. I need not again give you directions, as "FIELD MARSHAL" is the very thing; keep him in your eye, and if you do as well for me in other selections I will be well contented. I never saw so perfect a thorough-bred horse, of the size I want (15 hands), so adapted to race and carry the extra weight as this "FIELD MARSHAL" you bought from Mr. Briscoe for me.*

Yours faithfully,
J. TANNER.

* *Subsequent to this order,* Mr. TANNER *purchased* "MADRID," *in Turkey, and decided on limiting his outlay to him and* "FIELD MARSHAL."

From Captain McCraithe, *the Celebrated "Gentleman Rider."*
Lougloher, Cahir, Ireland.

My Dear Hunt,—Perhaps your plan of publishing the opinions of *public* men amongst your testimonials may have a good effect, as coming from those admittedly well versed in horses and their belongings. It may have a good effect on those, if any there be, who do not know what a practical fellow you are in all matters relating to Stud and Stable. If any man *knows* better than you about a horse, he must have discovered something relating to him not heard of him before now.

With an earnest wish for a thorough appreciation of your utility in the business you have adopted,

I remain, my dear Vere,
Ever your sincere old friend,
THOMAS McCRAITHE.

From M. Roberts Vanson.

Phaffendorf, near Ehrembrësten, Prussia.

Dear Sir,—This is written at your request, to state whether I am satisfied at your treatment to me when I sent my money to you to lay out to the best of your judgment for horses for me, such as I tell in my letter I want for me.

The horses you sent here to me from London are very good horses, and bought worth their money. If I were to buy them once more, I should not hesitate to pay the double of the money they costed me. Now, you satisfy me so much in all respects that I tell all my friends how Captain Hunt will do with them for English horses. The only thing I regret is that I did not take your advice at the time I bought two other horses in London; because I soon found the chesnut one is worth *nothing*, just as you said, while you were quite right of other one, the grey one, which is a most good horse, like those others you send me.

Yours, dear Sir, with consideration,
M. ROBERTS VANSON.

To Captain Hunt, London.

From The Comte de Marnix, "*Master of the Horse*" *to the King of Belgium.*

Bruxelles, 1864.

This is to certify I have employed Captain Hunt as his Majesty's agent for horse-buying in England, to purchase stallions and other horses for the Royal studs, and he has given complete satisfaction.

(Signed). CHAS. DECONE,
For The COMTE DE MARNIX.

From Mr. Charles Decone, *Assistant to The Comte de Marnix, Master of the Horse to the Belgium Court.*

14, Rue Montoyer, Quartier Leopold,
Bruxelles, *Sept. 4th,* 1861.

Dear Capt. Hunt.—I have seen the Count respecting the stallion you have for £400, but we will not have any more stallions from you, or any one else, this year. But hope next year that we shall do good business together again, as the Count has a very high opinion of you. He looks forward, with confidence in your judgment, to the receipt of the ten harness horses you say you will send here in November.

Yours, Captain, very respectfully,
CHARLES DECONE.

To Captain Hunt,
Warrington Stables, Maida Vale, London.

From the Master of the Tipperary Fox Hounds.

Wilford, Callan, Ireland.

My Dear Hunt.—From my knowledge of you since the time when, prior to the sale of your fine estate in this country, you hunted regularly, and in the *van guard* of the " Tips," I can have no objection, but, upon the contrary, great pleasure to give my opinion upon a subject that your clever and highly appreciative pen has long since made a matter generally known to the sporting and horse-keeping public, namely, that as a practical horse manager, a first-rate judge, and a clever salesman, not easily "done!" you have certainly no superior that I have ever met.

I remain, my dear HUNT,
Yours very truly,
JOHN GOING,
Master Tipperary Fox Hounds.

From the Most Noble The MARQUIS OF WATERFORD, *Master of Fox Hounds, Curraghmore.*

DEAR HUNT,—Dick Butler has asked me to write you a line as to my opinion of your competency for the arduous profession the loss of your estate has compelled you to adopt. From my long acquaintance with you, both when I hunted your county and since, I can say that you are thoroughly practical in horse matters, and that I have great faith in your birth and antecedents operating to preserve you in the only true road to success—perfect straightforwardness with the English public. I heartily wish you success. I like your *pluck* in not being beaten by *hard luck.*

Very faithfully yours,
WATERFORD.

From the Master of the Curraghmore Fox-Hounds.

Tinvane-Carrick-on-Suir,
2nd March, 1861.

DEAR SIR,—I have great pleasure in stating that I employed you to purchase me a stallion, for stud purposes, unseen by me, and upon your written description. I was very much pleased with him when he arrived from England, and your description was perfectly accurate, though cautious. You might with justice have recommended more highly than you did. Since this transaction I have been benefitted by your agency (you having sold "FIELD MARSHAL" for me at a "big figure"), and I have entrusted you with a commission for another stud horse, as I am well pleased with your agency, both selling and buying for me, and have implicit reliance in your good faith and unquestionably sound judgment.

I may add to this testimonial that I have known you for a long time as a highly respectable gentleman, representing one of the most honoured and aristocratic families in your native county, where you inherited a fine old seat and large property.

Believe me to be, dear Sir, faithfully yours,
HENRY W. BRISCOE,
Master Curraghmore Fox-Hounds.

From Sir RICHARD SUTTON, BART., *Master of Fox-Hounds.*

DEAR SIR,—I know you very well. I have enjoyed pleasant sport in your company in Ireland. I have great pleasure in bearing testimony to you as a gentleman, a good sportsman, and an unusually fine horseman, and judge of a horse.

Truly yours,
RICHARD SUTTON.

From Sir TATTON SYKES, Bart.

DEAR SIR,—You were introduced to me by Honourable Col. Cholmondley (my son-in-law), who said you were a good judge of horses. From your remarks and answers to my questions when inspecting my stud, I think so too.

Yours truly,
TATTON SYKES.

From the Master of Ludlow Fox-Hounds.

Ferny Hall,
Onibury, Salop.

DEAR SIR,—I purchased a horse, selected by you for me, from Mr. Bainbrigg, Woodseat, Ashbourne, Derby. I never saw the horse till he was my property and sent home. I have now hunted him for some time, and am much pleased with him.

Yours truly,
To Capt. HUNT.
W. H. SITWELL,
Master Ludlow Fox-Hounds.

From the Master of East Kent Fox-Hounds.

DEAR SIR,—I like the brown horse you so strongly recommended me, he is going on very well. I wish you would get me another, but I am in no hurry. I consider you a judge of a hunter.

Yours truly,
apt. HUNT.
T. BROCKMAN.

From Major-General SHIRLEY.

Brookside Lodge, near Rugby,
Jan. 15th, 1862.

DEAR SIR,—In answer to your letter, I have much pleasure in stating that I have a good opinion of your judgment in horses, and can certify to your having supplied me with a wonderful animal to carry weight and go a great pace with hounds; and I have seen *always* "judges' horses" in your stables, all evincing sound judgment in selection. I always think it requires a man *thoroughly experienced in riding to hounds* (like yourself) to be a reliable judge of a hunter.

I may add that I have *invariably* found you to be straightforward in all the many transactions that have taken place between us.

I am, yours very faithfully,
Captain HUNT.
ARTHUR SHIRLEY.

From Captain the Honourable A. D. S. DENISON, *Royal Navy.*

Yorkshire Club, 1869.

DEAR CAPTAIN HUNT,—I have got a ship and must be off to China on short notice. We have not much prospect of meeting again for years. I have given instruction for the sale by auction of my stud here. Perhaps you will have some friends you would wish those extraordinary good horses you have supplied me with to go into the hands of.

Believe me to be, with best wishes,
Very truly yours,
A. D. S. DENISON.

From Sir G. G. MONTGOMERY, Bart., M.P., &c., &c.

Stobo Castle, Stobo, N.B.
October 23rd, 1871.

SIR,—I enclose an advertisement I have just put in the Scotch papers in reference to the pair of horses I bought through your agency last July, and which I wish now to dispose of only because mine is a heavy carriage and the roads are hilly. I can warrant them to a purchaser in all particulars.

I am, yours truly,
G. GRAHAM MONTGOMERY.

From COLONEL COLVILLE, *Governor of County Middlesex Prison.*

Cold Bath Fields, W.C.
Dec. 19th, 1873.

Having purchased a horse for my brougham, selected by Captain Hunt, I certify that I am well satisfied with it; and that I believe him to be a trustworthy agent and a good judge of horses.

THOS. H. COLVILLE.

From Captain W. BELFIELD, *Pall Mall Club.*

Malmaury, Frenchay, Gloucestershire.
August 3rd, 1873.

DEAR CAPTAIN HUNT,—As regards the testimonial you ask me for, I can only say that the trouble you took to assist me in the matter of horses, and the patience, energy, and knowledge you displayed in procuring the same was to me highly satisfactory and commendable, as I have no doubt it will prove to others who will test your efficiency and *judge for themselves by experience* as I have done.

Believe me, faithfully yours,
W. BELFIELD.

From Sir JACOB HENRY PRESTON, Bart., *Beeston Hall, near Norwich.*

Beeston Hall,
Dec. 17th, 1873.

DEAR CAPTAIN HUNT.—I have much pleasure in stating that the carriage horses, hunter, and pony that you bought for me five or six years ago are still in my possession, and doing their work to my entire satisfaction.

Believe me, yours truly,
J. H. PRESTON.

From Captain Honourable A. D. T. DENISON, R.N., *Curzon Street, Mayfair.*

DEAR CAPTAIN HUNT,—I can truly say, out of the very many horses you have purchased me since 1867, I never had a bad one.

Yours very truly,
A. D. T. DENISON.

From the Rev. Canon GEO. PROTHERO, *Rector of Whippingham, Isle of Wight, and Chaplain to the Queen.*

Hora Bridge, Plymouth.
Sept. 23rd, 1873.

DEAR SIR,—I enclose you the letters sent me, and am glad to find that those who appear to know you best appreciate you. I am sure no one wishes you success more fervently than I do.

Yours very truly,
GEO. PROTHERO.

From Colonel THOS. H. COLVILLE, *Middlesex House of Correction.*

Cold Bath Fields,
Feb. 24th, 1874.

DEAR SIR,—I am glad to hear you are going on prosperously and giving satisfaction to customers. My horse continues to give satisfaction, and does credit to your choice.

Yours faithfully,
Captain DE VERE HUNT,   THOS. H. COLVILLE.
    Boscobel House,
        Regent's Park, N.W.

From J. S. GORDON, Esq., from Cape of Good Hope.

Woodside, Teddington.
Feb. 21st, 1874.

DEAR CAPTAIN HUNT,—It gives me the greatest pleasure in stating my entire approval of the manner in which you have so satisfactorily negotiated the purchase of the stallion LANGHAM for me for exportation; and that I shall be only too glad to recommend you to any friends of mine requiring the services of such an invaluable agency as yours.

I cannot refrain from adding that to the most keen and practical judgment in your operations on my behalf you have evinced a resolution in and capacity for hard work that fairly astounded me, and I must say you are the most indefatigable and hard-working man I ever had dealings with, and that I consider your charges reasonable, honest, and hardly earned.

I remain, yours obliged and sincerely,

Captain DE VERE HUNT,   J. S. GORDON.
    Boscobel House,
        Regent's Park, N.W.

[PERSONAL.]

Lismore School,
March 7th, 1855.

MY DEAR VERE,— You ask me for a letter in the shape of a testimonial, which you wish to be provided with for the furtherance of ulterior objects.
I feel much pleasure in stating that, in addition to a most excellent natural disposition, your literary attainments are sound and satisfactory; and that for a period of five years that you were resident pupil here, your conduct was unexceptionable.
I have had large pecuniary transactions with you since your arrival at man's estate, and am bound to say your treatment of me was highly satisfactory, and most honourable to yourself.
I remain, most affectionately,
Your sincere friend,
W. R. STOKES.

VERE HUNT, Esq.,
Clonhugh Park,
Co. Westmeath.

Howth Castle,
June, 1856.

MY DEAR SIR,—I have no objection to say (at your request) that the letters you have brought me, prior to obtaining a Commission in Lord St. Lawrence's Regt., are highly creditable to you, and from gentlemen of highest position in this county, including Mr. Hamilton, our M.P. Also that Mr. Quinn, of Loughloher Castle, and the Marquis of Waterford have specially spoken to me very favourably about you.
Your obedient servant,
HOWTH,
Lord-Lieut. Co. Dublin.

To VERE D. HUNT, Esq.,
Richmond Barracks, Dublin.

Shaubally Castle,
August 21st, 1855.

MY DEAR SIR,—I regret very much your application for a Company in the North Tipperary Regt. has come too late, all Captains' Commissions having been filled up. I admit your claims, and am fully aware of your high respectability, and the loyal service always done by your ancestors in my memory. I have only to express my regret that I have not what you require at my disposal, and, doubtless, you would decline subaltern rank.
Yours faithfully,
LISMORE,
Lord Lieutenant Co. Tipperary.

VERE D. HUNT, Esq.,
Clonhugh Park, Mullingar.

Lisfinney Castle,
Tallow, Co. Waterford.

MY DEAR HUNT,—I have known you from boyhood, when you were an inmate of Lismore School with my son Edward. Then I formed of you an exalted position, which, in your maturer years, I have had no reason to change. I can also say you were born to a fine portion and high position in your native county, of which untoward circumstances deprived you at the same crisis that ruined many of the first gentlemen of our land.
I remain, my dear Hunt,
Very sincerely yours,
EDWD. CROKER,
Brevet-Major.

VERE HUNT, Esq.
Clonhugh Park,
Mullingar.

Cashel.

MY DEAR SIR,—I beg to say I have known your family for upwards of seventy years, and have sat upon the Grand Jury of this County for upwards of thirty years with your grandfather, your father, and other members of your family—all known and respected for their superior culture and abilities.

Your grandfather I knew very well; he was one of the best High Sheriffs we ever had, and one of the most talented gentlemen at a critical period.

I have known yourself from the time you and my son Charles were little boys at school, and then, and now, we all thought, and think, very highly of you, both as an honourable man, a sincere friend, and a perfect gentleman.

You lost your fine property through the mis-management of others; and it being sold at a depressed period for such property, it did not realize half its value; and you, like many another high fellow, became the victim of circumstances.

I remain, very faithfully yours,
R. B. H. LOWE,
Deputy-Lieutenant Co. Tipperary.

Extract from a Letter in "TIMES" *Newspaper, Feb. 6th,* 1856.

"TO THE EDITOR OF THE 'TIMES.'

"SIR,—I saw Captain HUNT's name mentioned in your paper as having 'given assistance to the survivors from the wreck of the *Josephine Willis*, emigrant ship.' I am sure if you had seen the gallantry and heroic conduct displayed by that noble young fellow in the midst of death, and when it was supposed the vessel he was on board of was sinking, you would have extolled his self-sacrificing bravery in glowing terms. When comparative order was restored, I saw him administering comfort and consolation to the wretched survivors with a voice and manner kind and gentle as that of some tender woman.

"Who Captain HUNT is, I know not; but for his humanity and gallantry upon that dreadful night, may God Almighty bless his noble heart, is the prayer of

"A GRATEFUL SURVIVOR."

[LITERARY.]

OPINIONS OF THE PRESS.

"The Horse and his Master," by V. D. HUNT, Esq. [Longman],—is unexceptionably the most sensible little book we have met with, as to the diffusion of sound principles of Breeding, Training, and Stable Management. * * * * There is sound knowledge pervading the whole work, and every equestrian ought at once to procure and study it.—*John Bull*, May 21st, 1859.

"The Horse and his Master," with Hints on Breeding, Breaking, Stable Management, Training, Elementary Horsemanship, and Riding to Hounds, &c., by VERE D. HUNT, Esq. [Longman, p. 151.]—Another volume of "The Horse—horsey." It is a sensibly written treatise upon the nature of the horse, and the best means of breeding and managing it. Altogether a practical and very useful little manual.—*The Critic*, May 5th, 1859.

"The Horse and his Master," [Longman.]—Here is another contribution to what may be called the *equine literature* of the day. It is a treatise on Breeding, Breaking, and Stable Management of the Horse, by VERE DAWSON HUNT, Esq. The subject of breeding has been treated at great length and by the ablest writers (the author for one) in our columns; and there is little doubt that when the winter months shall put a stop to many of those sports, the details of which fill up the major portion of our columns, the subject will again be revived. In the mean time we have great pleasure in recommending this practical and very ably written little volume to all lovers of the animal; convinced as we are that it will foster and promote the feeling which is so rapidly gaining ground, that we have been for many years losing sight of some of the first principles of breeding—principles which now, more than ever, demand the earnest attention of all Englishmen.—*Bell's Life in London*, May 8th, 1859.

"The Horse and his Master," [Longman.]—The object of this very useful little manual is to afford hints on the Breeding, Breaking, and Management of the Horse, Training, Elementary Horsemanship, and Riding to Hounds, &c., all of which appear to be well worthy of consideration amongst those who give both time and attention to such pursuits. These hints are written in an easy, graceful, and comprehensive style, and certainly supply many facts which prove that much more may be done in the management of horses than has been generally attempted.—*Bell's Messenger*, May 14th, 1859.

"The Horse and his Master," [Longman,] by VERE D. HUNT, Esq.—We have read this very useful and instructive volume with much pleasure, and feel happy in recommending it as a very ably written and instructive work, for which the author deserves the support and thanks of not only those who keep and breed horses, but of the public at large. The Fox-Hunter will applaud Hints on Riding to Hounds, at the end of the volume.—*Freeman's Journal*, May 9th, 1859.

"The Horse and his Master," [London: Longmans.]—In a time when devotion to literature has become so general an object of the million, and when great competition for public notice debars access to the desired goal, save through the way of high excellence and distinguished merit, it is a very pleasing duty to extol any work whose individual worth attracts encomium and defies cavil. The volume under notice is written in a style that will be easily understood by the stableman, and highly appreciated by the man of letters—vigorous, minute, redundant, and engrossing. The most casual observer will detect the strong confidence of the author, notwithstanding the unobtrusive manner in which his opinions are advanced; and the perspicuity and logical precision with which his views are supported, give ample testimony of great practical experience of the subjects he handles, and affords gratifying evidence of a cultivated talent of no ordinary capacity. This manual is very useful, and deserving general public attention, at a time when a well-mounted Cavalry and efficiently-horsed Artillery should be a paramount consideration with every Englishman.—*The World*, May 28th, 1859.

[LETTERS IN TESTIMONY OF ABILITY AND SUCCESSFUL AUTHORSHIP.]

From MR. BLACKWOOD, *Proprietor of "Blackwood's Magazine," Edinburgh.*

Blackwood, Edinburgh,
Jan., 1860.

DEAR SIR,—Your paper on "Our National Sports" is amusing and instructive, and written in a style much more literary and pleasing than generally characterises sporting authorship. Indeed, so much pleased was I with its intrinsic merit, though not at all suited in subject to our Magazine, that I had very nearly decided upon its publication. A friend, however, overruled my views, and we have both decided on returning the MS., at the same time expressing our complete approval of it as a work of very decided merit, and only returned as being unsuited in subject.

Yours truly,
JOHN BLACKWOOD.

To CAPT. HUNT,
Dublin.

From LORD WILLIAM LENNOX, *Editor of " The Review."*

4, Porchester Terrace, Hyde Park,
London, *April* 4th, 1859.

DEAR SIR,—I have much pleasure in stating that, since I have been Editor of "The Review," your contributions have been exceedingly valuable. Unlike other authors, you furnish "copy" in good time, and I have never had to call upon you to add or erase a single line.

Wishing you success in your literary career, and an open field for display of talents which must, if opportunity offers, raise their possessor to a high position amongst the sons of genius,

I remain, my dear Sir,
Very faithfully yours,
WILLIAM P. LENNOX.

CAPT. DE VERE HUNT.

From PROFESSOR CAMERON, *Editor of "The Agricultural Review."*
Office of Agricultural Review and Country Gentleman's Paper,
7, Great Brunswick Street, Dublin,
July, 1859.

I have great gratification in saying that CAPT. DE VERE HUNT, as Sporting Contributor and Reporter to this paper, has given very general satisfaction; and, I am bound to add, his productions in our columns and those of contemporaries have induced a large number of our subscribers.

C. A. CAMERON.

CAPT. DE VERE HUNT.

From Editor of Bell's Life," A.D. 1860.
Bell's Life Office, London,
March, 1860.

DEAR SIR,—Your request for a letter in the shape of a testimonial is unusual; all your contributions to the "*Life*" having been prominently inserted and paid for at our highest scale of remuneration, is surely the best test of your efficiency as a Sporting Writer.

I may add your contributions under the *nom de plume* of "SHAMROCK" have received general and well-merited notice of a complimentary character.

Yours very truly,
WILLIAM H. LANGLEY,
Editor.

From Editor of "Bell's Life," A.D. 1871.
Bell's Life Office, 1871.

DEAR SIR,—Your article upon The Horse, which I return, is *extremely well written*, and would make an admirable chapter for a book on the subject. But in its present form, it is unsuited to my views as to what ought to be provided for the *reader of to-day*. For a newspaper, as a rule, I consider continuous chapters objectionable, as being more suited to magazine literature.

If, however, you choose to resume the thread of your discourse upon "OUR RE-MOUNTS AND GENERAL HORSES," I shall be very pleased to give your contributions prominent insertion, as heretofore.

I am, my dear Sir, faithfully yours,
HENRY SWAITHWAITE,
Editor *Bell's Life.*

Vide "Waterford Mail."—July 6th, 1860.

Our Sporting Columns have, since the recent extension of matter in our paper, contained original contributions and reports calculated to interest that portion of our readers having a *penchant* for the turf and field sports generally. And as we are determined to cater for our constituents, regardless of expense, we have engaged a gentleman of established literary fame in *equine* and general sporting writing (standard and periodical), to produce our sporting news in that form of high excellence for which he is so pre-eminent.

In introducing "SHAMROCK" of *Bell's Life in London* as the gentleman above alluded to, we give the best guarantee to our readers that our hopes and encomiums are reasonable and just.

Hibernian Magazine Offices,
7, Wellington Quay, Dublin,
July 14th, 1860.

MY DEAR SIR,—I duly received the MS. you kindly sent me, and although the terms you have named are higher than I have paid heretofore, I do agree to them, as I know your articles are of the highest literary merit, and in my opinion the sum you have named is not too much. Mediocre articles I always thought too dear for me at any price.

Yours very truly,
JAMES DUFFY.

www.ingramcontent.com/pod-product-compliance
Lightning Source LLC
Chambersburg PA
CBHW032154160426
43197CB00008B/909